THE PENDULUM

THE PENDULUM

by

ANTHONY ROSSITER

LONDON
VICTOR GOLLANCZ LTD
1966

PRINTED IN GREAT BRITAIN
BY EBENEZER BAYLIS AND SON, LTD.
THE TRINITY PRESS, WORCESTER, AND LONDON

For Anneka

Victory may indeed be achieved over what has been experienced, and yet that experience is still in our possession as a permanent enhancement and extension of the reality of our spiritual life. What has once been lived through cannot possibly be effaced. That which has been continues to exist in a transfigured form. Man is by no means a completely finished product. Rather he moulds and creates himself in and through his experience of life, through spiritual conflict, and through those various trials which his destiny imposes upon him. Man is only what God is planning, a projected design.

Berdyaev

It is good for us at times to have troubles and adversities; for often they make a man enter into himself, so that he may know that he is in exile, and may not place his hopes in anything of this world.

The Imitation of Christ
Chapter XII, Verse 1

PREFACE

This book, which has changed continuously in its unflowering, tells of some experiences over eighteen years which I think to be of interest, and at times of importance.

The events, situations, experiences and results which are the substance of this story are intended to be seen as a whole.

I am emphatic, if about nothing else, that this story be understood as a growth, a progression through a wide variety of experiences which, anyway to me, make some sense. I have discovered much, for and about myself, during the growth of this book, and it is my hope that at least some of these discoveries have filtered into the pages.

As I correct the proofs, a good example comes to mind. Opposite me is a simple household radiator. It speaks to me, now, with the authority of Kipling's 'If'.

The radiator system around the walls which had once been liquid molten lead is frozen static—still—now conveying through its stillness heat around.

I have discovered, perhaps most important of all, that there are infinite ways of looking at everything, be it a pear, a painting, a person or a problem.

It just depends what you want.

My hope is that in understanding these pendulumonic experiences, I may in the future convert them to gyroscopic advantage.

A. R.
Litton, February 1966.

Part 1

CHAPTER ONE

"'ERE'S YER KNIFE, fork, spoon and sope—what's yer religion?"
This was my greeting at the Guards Depot at Caterham, in company with many other eighteen-year-olds a few weeks before the
Invasion of Europe. For some months we were to find stressed,
in the Brigade of Guards, the close link between cleanliness and
godliness. To have a button missing on Church Parade was, in
the words of the Regimental Sergeant Major, "to be naked in the
'ouse of God".

A year later, with a gold-peaked hat tilted correctly forward
over my eyes, I saw, not entirely clearly, the gates leading into
Sandown Park and reported as an Ensign to the Training Battalion
of the Welsh Guards. It was here that I had the first indications of
what later was to prove to be the pendulum. Where horses now
stand pawing the ground, Sergeants had their billets. The stables
then housed more men than the Jockey Club would permit horses
these days and the course itself was scattered with huts, wire,
carriers, tanks and all the paraphernalia of an army. The Tote was
the Officers' Mess, and the draught there was terrific: the table-
cloth was often held in place by heavy Regimental silver. It was a
strange room but not without its compensations; the company
was good, the talk centred on art more than on the usual army
business, and the walls were decorated with some paintings by
Rex Whistler. It was a civilised and friendly atmosphere. We
were mainly amateur soldiers and many were much interested in
art. I remember my months ar Sandown as happy ones, both for
the way I was tolerated as a very amateur soldier and for the vivid
talks we had about art and creative matters. In fact the first thing
my Company Commander said to me when I reported to him
was: "You're Rossiter, aren't you? Very keen on painting . . .
Well, that's marvellous, you must come and see my collection

when we're in Wales." The Mess was full of interesting people, there was a strong sense of belonging to a very select club. And I was commissioned: this had surprised both me and the very loud shouting Sergeant Major who had 'trained me' and had inflicted upon me the first of my nervous twitches.

I set about my work dead keen, earnest and I think rather over-conscientious. I was determined to prove myself a worthy soldier, fit for my smart hat and a credit to the Regiment. I found life increasingly exciting and stimulating. I had been immediately impressed, on joining up at Caterham, by the Guards' drilling, the impressive display of men on parade. I was shorter than the average Guardsman, but even if my heart was a few inches lower than the rest, it was in the right place. The drill, the discipline, the massed parades, the almost edible hats, the blancoing, the glinting bayonets and shining buckles, and the classic precision of the movements around me, moved me deeply.

Order came firmly into my life with the delivery of commands. But it was not the power of these commands which delighted me, where my merest word would change the whole architectural conception set before my eyes; rather it was the visual perfection of the sight and its inevitability which gave wing to my imagination. I rose with the rifles as they leapt, as if by magic, from thigh to shoulder level, perfect in their click and vertical ascent. And as they thundered on to a hundred shoulders, diagonalled to the sky, my mind was bayonetted sharply upwards. To be able to relax the same lines of forward-tilted grounded rifles with just two words, 'Stand Easy', and instantly to see a perfection of tautness vanish into eased arms, was nothing short of a miracle to me.

The total masculinity of army life held me in its grip. In particular I sensed the authority which belts and buckles held. The Sam Browne which I so proudly wore was something more than just a highly polished belt and diagonal strap. Wearing it stamped me with more than just authority; it was a seal of certainty. As I threw this symbol of my authority into a chair, relaxing in my room, I was suddenly stripped of much more than a mere darkly polished belt. Gone was my authority, my firm words of command, my masculinity. I realised then, for the first time, the importance of uniform and all it symbolises.

Life at Sandown soon raised me to heightened perceptions, so delighted was I by all I saw and experienced. The stars on officers' shoulders glinted more miraculously than those which peeped through the suburban sky above our Surrey household. Shining polished toe caps gleamed more fiercely than sunset lights upon the Thames. And in the mess, those glowing hats hung so nonchalantly on pegs spoke clearly (and in the same voice) of privilege and authority. Little did I realise that this highly disciplined community, of which I was such an earnest member, would be the setting for an experience so lacking in these qualities of order, balance and discipline, that within a year my polished pride would be more than rubbed into the earth, it would be bundled and bound up in a strait-jacket.

I was becoming more and more stimulated by the things I saw around me. I felt in full fettle, ready for anything. And in my spare time I was browsing round picture galleries for the first time in my life. At the National Gallery, where the war artists exhibited their work and where the concerts of Myra Hess still echoed, I found contact with painters whom I had only known before from reproductions: Eric Ravilious, Paul Nash, the scratched lines of Piper's scarred walls, the dark gutted East End street of a Sutherland drawing. In many of these paintings I found expression of the forces struggling for release within me. In particular I remember the impact of Henry Moore's shelter drawings, expressing man's adaptability in times of stress; these contrasted savagely with Renoir's exquisite young girl in 'La Loge', which hung as the 'picture of the month', alone in the hall, reminding one that life had another side, even if it was temporarily submerged.

Esher was my home at that time, for all officers (except the Adjutant and Picquet Officer) were billeted in the town. At first I lodged in a luxurious modern house on a large estate, a private bathroom next to my bedroom; this was ready at any hour of the day to be drawn for me by my servant, who would not only fill it to the correct level but also sprinkle bath salts into it, so that it was, anyway on the surface, an immaculate young Guards officer who would then appear, ready for further training in combat, self-defence and the leading of his platoon into the bloody fields of battle. But it was not long, on the battle course, before the effects of the bath salts wore off. Life was a happy, and ironic, mixture of ease and spartan toughness, which appealed to the duality of my nature.

I found the town a little smug; this is something which I always feel about smart suburbia, where almost too perfect houses, and their inhabitants, spell to me a falseness. At that time I was quite content to accept their pattern of life, but underneath I sensed something which was not part of me; or, to put it another way, was perhaps so nearly a part of me that I shied away from it. I found in these houses expensive reproductions of famous works of art, usually the Impressionists, but I understood clearly that their owners knew little about the faith and courage that had made those paintings possible; and I sensed that these reproductions were decorations rather than an integral part of their owners' lives.

The streets themselves were complacent too. The public house where a few of us sometimes drank was no longer really public; indeed, it was most private in its buttoned-and-crested-jacket exclusiveness; but I sometimes joined this fraternity, leaning forward as my drinking companions did to pip a 'dirty story', and with the ensuing laughter my ego and self-confidence were boosted. Again, even at nineteen, I found in this pub world something which was not really me. But in my lack of confidence I needed to be accepted, both in that world and in the Guards' mess. Looking back over the years, and over my more recent experiences, I realise now that it was at Sandown, soon after my arrival there, that the pendulum first swung too high, just for a short time. The experience was strange at the time, but not really alarming, for I put it down to fatigue, which in some respects it was.

I remember going to a party in London, thoroughly enjoying myself, and returning to Esher in the early hours of the morning. I had drunk very little; at that time, in such a healthy and fit state, I did not feel the need of drink, either to stimulate or relax me. Back at Esher I set off, in high spirits, to find my digs for a few hours' rest before morning parade.

But I began to wander through those tempting streets. I must have walked the streets of Esher for some six hours. I was floating, unable to meet the reality of finding the little suburban house in which I lodged. Many times I pushed open a small wooden gate and marched up the narrow path to find a door which was not quite my own. Something was different, something was out of place and not connected with the door for which I searched. The image of the door was drawn upon my mind but it was so much confused by other thoughts that it was not possible to isolate and retain it. And when I encountered some new house, which this time must be mine, the image again eluded me and my mind danced with a thousand other thought associations. Joy changed to panic as dawn slowly turned the streets from dark, suggestive shapes to objects which I clearly recognised and which were no longer part of a dream. The last gate I had gently closed had become green and almost ready for its daily task. I was seized with panic at the sight of a garden trowel, dug into a patch of earth; the owner might be watching me from behind lace curtains. I was lost, entirely lost, and as luminous and yet as incidental as the ochre stone which rested on a window sill. It seemed to stare back at me, mocking. What connection was there between me, in my blue patrol uniform and gold-peaked hat, and this slowly awakening street? How could I slip into this early morn, inconspicuously and find a place in a world of which I no longer was a part? Sweat filled the palms of my hands. Which way to turn? I turned down a small side avenue, and there, quietly, with dry amusement, stood the house in which I lodged. I rushed up to the lattice gate and my hands fumbled with the catch. Once in my room, my panic vanished. My sketching easel gave fine welcome and it was good to be with my books again. A discarded shirt linked me to the previous evening. Warmth filled my heart as I noticed the worn patch in the carpet. My hair brushes neatly paired together gave smug approval from the dressing table. A clean bath towel welcomed me in a rough and friendly manner. Everything in the room seemed pleased to see me and my mind took flight again as I glanced through my sketch book. As I undressed, so I discarded completely the panic which had enveloped me in that suburban street, and I sank happily into a bath, free of rank, fears and doubts.

I do not know how long I remained dreaming away in that bathroom; but it must have been quite some time. There was a knock on the door. A sergeant had been sent to the house by the Adjutant, to demand why I was not on parade. It was nine-thirty a.m. I remember my embarrassment. It brought me quickly to my senses. The door between us was more than just a wooden division, it was a symbol of the barrier between the world of imagination and that of the army. I understood clearly the seriousness of the situation, a sergeant, fully clothed and probably standing stiffly to attention, conveying a message to a completely naked young officer. The scene was funny only on the music halls. Here in Esher it would not do. The part of me which was ready to break into laughter was quickly stifled by thoughts of court martial proceedings, public ignominy, and the withdrawal of a sword which I had, alas, never owned. I would be stripped of authority in public, for being stripped too long in private. My voice quivered as I replied to the sergeant. I excused myself on account of sickness and sent a message that I would be taking the remainder of the day off. "Sir!" came the prompt reply from the sergeant as he stamped to attention on the other side of the door, I imagine at the salute, and the soap jumped off the edge of the bath in fright. I heard him turn on his heel—one stop, two stop, three stop—there was another vibrating thud as the right foot sharply rejoined the left, and he was gone. I was left alone, fishing for the soap in a cloudy and well cooled bath, feeling very stupid.

There is no doubt that that was my first meeting with the pendulum; it had swung for a short time too high and I had been out of contact with reality. The military invasion of that small landing outside the bathroom had soon brought me to my senses. My feet were firmly on the mat, and upon the ground, as I hurriedly dried myself down with the rough bath towel. But I realised clearly that I had only just avoided being truly 'on the mat'. Suffice to say I was neither court-martialled nor shot and after a day's rest the pendulum resumed its normal rhythm.

CHAPTER TWO

THE JOURNEY WHICH eventually landed me in Greece was taken via a route to which the War Office gave some fantastic initials; route ULNA or was it USTY?—I just cannot remember. "You came by USTY did you?" was a common question in the Middle East at that time. "Indeed I did," I probably answered rather pompously; but these bare initials can give no possible indication of the thrilling nature of the journey.

I remember first the magic of the white foam on the side of the ship whilst crossing the Channel. I sniffed, on board the boat, as a fresh young horse does on an early morning exercise on the downs. The freedom and sparkling freshness of the French countryside, as it flashed past, contrasted vividly with the distorted khaki shapes which interwove themselves in all the carriages, sprawling and linked together in fatigue. In Toulon time had come to a standstill, and the camp which gave us little welcome, either in gesture or appearance, reflected the emptiness of victory. The practical and ugly concrete buildings, now stripped of urgent activity and strife, stood ironically apart. The prostrated figure of a drunk young officer, flat out on an army bed, was a comment on the rusted hulls of the scuttled ships in the harbour.

The elegant white horizontal rails of the ship which took us from Toulon to the Middle East brought to that journey a special peace. It was a world of horizontals, rails and horizon, broken by the positive verticality of masts and funnels. Light played magic games upon the decks and the shadow from a life-boat would encompass a group of card-playing men; then quite suddenly it would shift an inch, and a card would gleam white against the dark shadow and an arm would glisten. We turned from white to brown on that calm sunlit voyage, a floating island of men temporarily relieved of responsibility. I remember the whiteness of my life jacket and its contrast to my darkening skin. To inspect a 'Guard' in this pregnant attire was, for me, the height of absurdity. As my stuffed one-piece breast almost caressed that of the men before me, I experienced a strange sort of love, a love born of absurdity, circumstance and fact. Our contact was made the greater, not only by our swollen size, but by the intimate circumstances of our dual adventure out there in the middle of the ocean. If we were to sink, which one of us would really float and keep alive this pretence of rank? The puffed pride of officers was ridiculed in this life-saving attire, in which we were made equals in shape and absurdity. The ocean, if it did test us, would prove our rank and worth. The best penguin would soon exhibit his better self.

My mind was keenly tuned to such matters and delighted by the white of rail against the ultramarine of sea. The stripped wood of decks, freshly washed in the early morning, tempted me to run my hand along them and smooth them even more. Against these cool strips of wood, bronzed men would glow and sweat and sleep. On occasion a pendant identity disc, dark and round, would linger for a moment embraced by glistening hairs on a bare chest; then it would fall into a vertical position, out of the embrace, as the owner leaned forward to play his ace. We glided, glowing and glistening, over that impersonal ocean, imprisoned in an ark which had collected few of the opposite sex.

When we landed at Port Said I was reminded of the time when I had entered a miniature aeroplane, in the toy department of a large London store, and had stepped out into a new world a few minutes later. Suddenly, without memory of passing scenes, here I was in another world, where crafty boats glinted in the sunlight, and black faces glowed darkly from persil-white shrouds. A land of half veils and the suggestiveness which is engendered by such calculated reticence.

The train which took us painfully across Egypt, from Port Said to Cairo, seemed to be made of skin tautly drawn over thin bones. It matched the scrabbling and emaciated fowls which decorated the roofs of white rectangular concrete houses, boxes joined by a sea of rubble and excreta. I stared with horror at these buildings and the filthy sights surrounding them, keeping my hands deeply in my pockets lest I touch any part of the train which was linked to these distasteful scenes. I wondered how human beings could eat and drink a few inches below such a sea of excreta and foulness.

The full heat of Egypt, baked like a turd, enveloped me when we arrived in Cairo. It was a relief to move out to our camp away from the city, to a flat expanse punctuated by neat white triangular tents. It was strange to unpack my belongings in this nomad home and to notice the markings of a Mayfair bootmaker as I unwrapped a new pair of shoes. There was no link between these assured and sophisticated markings and this world of sand, tents, Arabs and burning heat. The glare of the desert sprang up at me and struck me between the eyes. The Sphinx, the Pyramids, the ageless, limitless desert, all these were tempering my imagination.

I almost laughed when I first saw the Pyramids. Their certainty and force, their sheer audacity, their geometric simplicity, forced themselves straight into my mind. My eyes and mind shot up the triangle and clashed with full force at the apex, so that all my emotions were thundered at one point. And on return, down the diverging perfectly matched lines, I felt the full weight of every stone and man who were part of this eternal pyramid. Man, in architectural symbol, could never again be so positively certain.

I dined once at Shepheard's; and it was here that I first realised the gulf between extreme wealth and poverty. Part of me was ashamed at the liking I possessed for luxury, ease and comfort. This feeling of guilt faded after a few drinks, and as I gazed into the veined ice-cubes in my glass, I too became part of the world which the impermanence of the blocks in my glass symbolised.

On to Palestine, to the New Testament, a different glare, a different mood. Immediately I sensed its tragedies, its humiliations, its courage, its inevitability.

The Sea of Galilee is just as you imagine it, Capernaum, now probably less busy than in the days of Christ, as haunting as its name suggests. To ride on horseback up Mount Hermon, as we did in the very early morning, before the sun rose fully, and then drink pure orange juice from a cold clear glass and bathe an hour later in Galilee, this indeed was magic. Palestine, as it then was, was at its spring best, trees and shrubs blossoming; the heat of the sun had not had time as yet to scorch everything to stillness. I remember ploughed fields as rich as Cornish ones and trees bursting as in Somerset orchards.

I also remember the ironic contrast between our comforts and the stern tragedies around us. Our boating jackets, five glistening buttons on each cuff, and our smart blue dress-hats, were strangely out of place in a land fighting for the smallest privilege, the privilege of just living and working in a land free of terror. Away down there in the valley were camps into which were sneaking Jewish refugees from Europe under cover of the night.

And then to Greece, back in time to the golden age of art, architecture and philosophy. I remember becoming so blasé that I read Agatha Christie on the steps of the Parthenon. The sky, at this moment a deep azure blue, with the classical columns standing out against it, soon became overcast with dark thunder clouds as the storm approached. The tempo was rising, I was absorbing buildings, mosaics, landscapes, stories, museums, and fresh experiences hitherto undreamed of. My days, visually, were fully loaded. I received images as a camera does, but had little chance for 'developing the prints'. My mind was full of ideas, images and messages. I longed to print them, to expose them to others, to shout aloud my intense joy, to sing. This was almost impossible in army life, and at the time most of my companions were philistine. All save one: Colly, my senior in age and rank, became my 'tutor' and we shared many delightful hours together. Our meetings were alas too rare.

I had so much to sing about and was quite unable to transmit these songs into painting, already my natural means of expression.

I tried writing, it certainly helped at the time, though I am thankful that there is now no record of what I wrote. I remember it as a lot of sentimental nonsense. But it was a temporary outlet to my steaming mind.

As my mind began to boil, images that I had thought quite forgotten began to stir. Out of the pot came memories of childhood, Eton and my days at Sandown Park. These I tried to record in my writings, scribbling away at my desk late into the night. A pram which I had seen in the street one afternoon had started these recollections. It had been reflected in a window, some of its shiny blackness lost in the second image. I thought to call my book 'Reflections through a Window', partly because of this scene and partly because I could look out from my room in the mess on to a yard with just one tree in it, and often a slender pretty schoolgirl would be playing in it. Her youthful beauty and freshness and the way in which she leapt over her skipping rope reflected to perfection the zestful joys which were vibrating within me. Her slim bare legs were strangely fair in a country where most limbs were darkly tanned. They contrasted dramatically with the short dark skirt she often wore; and the pale rope flicked her legs upwards, missing the soles of her feet by just a fraction. She and the rope were lithe partners in a song of ecstasy. And so my mind skipped back to my youthful days, to days before sex had predominantly altered my way of thinking and I could delight, without greedy need of action, in sensual sights and feelings.

Back to a pram which I was helping to push at the age of three. I remembered this pram and the shiny black waterproof cover which was stretched across it when rain was near. And the day when I had been playing cricket, perhaps at the age of four, with the back of a park chair. I had handed the 'bat' to my brother and was playing wicket-keeper. Suddenly there were stars and blood and tears. The world was blurred and I was in pain. I remembered sitting in a sort of dentist's chair, there were nurses near at hand, and a man who looked a little like my father was doing something to my lip. There followed days when my mouth would only partially open and into it were fed small morsels of food. Mastoid days, bandages clinging to my head and my eyebrows lost beneath them. A turbanned world on top and faltering feet below, the cord of my dressing-gown reins for the nurse to hold. Lumps of sugar neatly arranged on a glass shelf above my bed. A lift descending to the fierce lights above a seemingly large-sized ironing board, on which I was laid, with soothing voices which trebled my dismay. Gas meant something especially terrible to me, something much more frightening than the pain which, at times, linked both my ears in a white-hot bar of steel. The ache of tight screwed nuts throbbed in the pit of those dark holes. Up into the red rubber sphere I rose, suffocating in panic, and down into a great black chasm I swiftly whirled, a tall black pointed witch's hat funnelling me down and down. Down down down, until it was all over and I awoke to a world of light echoed in the bright bandages around my head.

Eton; I tried in my writing to evoke the scent of autumn evenings on the playing fields when fog would disguise all but a few large shapes and I was young and sure and bold. And how my sureness had been turned to uncertainty and fear and a longing to be loved and liked.

Sitting on the steps of the Parthenon, I remembered a film which I had seen in Esher, a travelogue which had called it, 'the gateway into the classic past'. The gateway into the classic past! I compared the green wooden gate, which I had so hurriedly unlatched in Esher on that early morn, with the pillars which rose far above my head, crowned by a pediment of stone. Two suns spun in mind, the one constructed into the upper half of that Esher gate, the other lighting a land in glory and burning new messages into sculptured stone. As the sun dictates the time and shadow-shape upon a sun dial, so did this blazing light bring new meaning to these effigies which changed with every moving hour. It was a million miles from the prim suburban shadows to these three-dimensional echoes of Gods and men.

The pendulum swung sharply one very sunny morning, of all places in the cookhouse. I remember that I was inspecting the cookhouse, my duty as Picquet Officer of the day. Normally this was a very ordinary duty, with a touch of homeliness and humour: I do not think that army cooks took young officers, with obviously no culinary experience, very seriously. But on this particular morning my head began to swim as soon as I entered the building. The place was spotless, a model army cookhouse. Pots, pans, urns, shining ladles, suddenly became something quite different, divorced from their utilitarian purposes. I sensed a transcendental state of glory in that Greek-cum-British cookhouse on that divinely sunny morning, with shapes as perfect and organised as a Chardin. I stood dumbfounded by the door, hypnotised by it all. A particular ladle beckoned me. Part of my mind was saying, "Steady, old chap, you're on Picquet Duty in the kitchens, inspect it all calmly, do your duty." The other more insistent part was saying, "Damn the army and its cookhouse . . . just look at that urn and that magnificent array of white jugs . . . and look at that tureen, it would send old Chardin spinning". On this particular sunny inspection morning I realised, perhaps for the first time, the full profundity of art. I became a potential artist and lost any hope of becoming a Field Marshal.

I stood for what seemed hours in the doorway. My Sergeant coughed and made some remark to the point. But still I could not really bring myself to inspect this fantastically inspiring place. Another strange sensation was that though I was 'swimming', yet my vision was as clear as crystal. To this day, through a haze of a billion objects, scenes, events, I can still picture that Chardin-like cookhouse. On my left was an enormous copper urn, four times the size of the ones used in the pavilions of village cricket teams. Or so it seemed. It was both comforting and awe-inspiring. Objects immediately took on human character, the urn seemed to stand guard amongst more inferior people. A row of white jugs appeared delightfully pompous, spoons, the large ones, inviting and solicitous. A large brown jug looked the proudest person I had ever seen. The objects glowed from within, stood firm, and really were my friends. I loved them all.

I tried to make the inspection round the cookhouse. I believe I actually got round the whole set of rooms, but the journey was in a haze. I was beginning to lose my grip and enter another world. My mind was working at lightning speed, but only in one direction, towards the 'beatification' of all that surrounded me, away from army life. I remember dismissing my Sergeant and telling him that I would be in the Mess if he required me; and then I made my way there, as quickly as possible, to assess the situation. I particularly wanted to avoid meeting anyone. I closed the door of my room, just off the main Mess, quietly, and stood staring around me. Was I going mad? Everything in my room had the same distinction and appeal as the objects in the cook-house. It was a modest army room but full of things I loved, my desk piled high with cuttings and photographs, books, drawings, some ceramics. There was a cricket bat in the corner (how aristo-cratic it looked). The room was scarcely a typical army room; it had, in fact, the makings of a studio; several of my later studios were to echo the form of this room, where everyday objects which I loved surrounded me. In this Grecian sunlit room the objects seemed all to have a deep significance. I loved them; and they returned my love.

In a corner was a black paraffin stove, and a white washbowl close to a vase of flowers: the most radiant flowers I had ever seen. There was a strange deep harmony between the flowers and the black stove; they were in perfect communion. The flowers were white and yellow; full of glory, singing to each other. My dress-ing-gown hung from the door. A grey flannel one made from an army blanket. It had red facings. Now it was transformed into an agonised Crucifixion, its arms, caught on other hooks, out-stretched. There was the Crucifixion in its entirety. I remember kneeling down and praying. This was some God-sent moment, He was about to reveal himself. I must wait and listen.

It is worth digressing at this point to say that often at the height of the pendulum swing, imaginings stem of a religious nature. The world around you is full of revelations. This is an important point; the essence of the revelations may not be what it might seem to be at the time, God-sent messages to oneself, marching orders as it were, but they are nevertheless revelations. Much is revealed to you in such a state, much that it is impossible to record, not because it would sound too fanciful or too fantastic, but because mere words are inadequate. The point which Gerard Manley Hopkins makes is so true; "the world is charged with the Grandeur of God".

I seemed to read messages in chairs, stoves, tables, pots, pans, flowers, in anything. It is the way in which you act upon this revelation which determines your sanity. If you see these messages as inspirational ideas, contacts with deeper realities, symbols of the mystic values of life, you are using them correctly, as symbols expressing something greater than themselves. If you kneel down in front of a dressing-gown crucifixion, you are very near insanity, harmless as it may be. Many an artist, poet, writer, thinker must have stumbled upon this, and even knelt, but many more have arisen, taken their cross with them, and plodded on in life. It took me many years to learn this, to accept these symbols, and high-flown imaginings, and to use them without danger to my everyday life.

But I was very young, miles from home and my friends, and in a truly 'high' state. The pendulum was swinging viciously and there was no one to whom I could turn. I turned consequently to my dressing-gown, the paraffin stove and white washbowl. They seemed to know all the answers. They became my objects of love and inspiration, my last sources of contact. I would draw them and unravel further truths. I got out my pencils, and set out on a frenzy of drawing, during which many things were to happen. My pencils raced across the paper as if magically guided.

I drew with great concentration and energy. My pencil danced over the paper, scouring it with scrawls and swirls. I scarcely looked at the paper; my gaze was concentrated on the objects around me. I was furiously recreating the stove, and whilst I drew, the stove changed from one mood to another. What had started as a fine, upright, proud, black stove turned into a prancing teapot, then back to a stove less sure of itself, which said (I inscribed the words below), "Which way now?" My paper darkened as the scrawls increased. My dressing-gown, usually so calm and limp upon its hook, took on the passionate forms of the Crucifixion and the Flagellation, 'close to Christ', and expressing to me the whole sorrow of the world. As exhaustion overcame me, I was no longer drawing a dressing-gown but spinning in a world of inward agony and deep suffering, sensing Christ's Agony in the Garden of Gethsemane.

I drew on sheet after sheet. Later I discovered that I had used the back of a pile of printed army orders. I would tear a sheet from the pile and begin another whilst the last one fluttered to the floor. I was lying on my bed working at a concentrated pitch hitherto unknown. The room darkened, evening was approaching, and still I drew. Then, utterly exhausted, I lay back on my pillow and slept, awakening to a dark room and a sea of drawings ebbing round the bed.

I scarcely dared to move. Despite the sleep I was still in an ecstatic state. Carefully I climbed off the bed and collected the drawings, arranging them in order on the floor, a whole exhibition of passionate drawings, many with words beneath them such as 'Which Way Now?', 'Uncertain Stove', 'The Teapot said or was it the stove?', 'Complete Chaos', 'Not such a certain bowl'. I do not remember inscribing these words, they were part of the search in these drawings. I was proud of the array of drawings, probably about twenty in all. I must have worked for several hours without stopping and longed to work some more. I lit the paraffin fire and started again—the objects on my desk, the white washbowl, two wrestling towels, a proud bucket, a despairingly empty armchair. I must have continued for a further couple of hours before I was disturbed by my servant knocking on the door. He was carrying a tray of food and looked concerned. I explained that I did not feel well and just wanted to stay in my room for a day or two. It did not occur to me to explain further or enquire why he had brought me this tray. I asked not to be disturbed further that evening and was left alone to my supper and a further bout of drawing which stretched far into the night, probably another fifty drawings, all animated and compelled by an inner driving force over which I had virtually no control. I was immensely happy whilst my pencil scrawled its symbols across the pages, oblivious of time and space. It was essential, in some way, to record the messages morsing from my mind, to translate them on to paper. I remember the force with which I drew, the power and rhythms which were concentrated, the temporary emotional release which they gave. And in between I would kneel for some few minutes before my dressing-gown and give thanks to God for this sublime 'moment', this inspiration and power to work. It was as if the secrets of the world had been unfolded to me, all of them, and I was walking with God in the Garden of Eden. The world around me no longer existed. Sleep, very poor sleep, overcame me at last; I dozed till morning, until my servant again appeared. The room was littered with drawings; I suddenly felt embarrassed. I explained that just another day in bed would do me good; no, I did not want to see a doctor, I was perfectly all right; I just wanted to work and be left alone.

A little later that morning a doctor was sent to see me. I did not realise he was a doctor for some time; I somehow accepted him, and his searching questions, as part of this God-sent plan. I talked freely with him, even when I realised his profession, though I now remember that my talk was punctuated with a sort of stuttering, my sentences not exactly appearing as I had shaped them. Again I explained that I just wanted a further day in which to work. When he left me, I dressed and a certain panic overcame me. I somehow felt I must get out and see a friend of mine. But I was terrified of leaving the sanctuary of my room. Gingerly I opened the door. There was no one about. I was sure they were all discussing me; suddenly I realised that I was behaving rather oddly. My first real dose of paranoia closed in on me. I escaped from the building, somehow, and walked in a dazed fashion towards where my friend Colly lived. By chance I met the doctor who had seen me in my room. Was it chance? Was I being watched? I scarcely lingered talking with him but hurried on, in a nightmare of fear, to the building at the other end of the town. My friend was out. I met several more acquaintances, dared not talk with them too long, and began my journey home in great haste, my paranoical fears increasing with each step. Whom would I meet next? What should I say to them? Would they see that something was wrong? I longed for my room, to close the door and settle down again amidst those well-loved objects. My pace hastened and I sped up to my room with silent movements, for fear of disturbing anyone. I closed the door with immense relief, undressed and got into bed. Here I felt safe, with my drawing-pad and pencil next to me. Ready for the next messages and signs, the next instalment of His Message. And so I drew again, at the same fevered tempo and with immense force.

I cannot remember the exact details of the next few days; perhaps the whole period, before I was hospitalised, was only a further day; but I do remember certain incidents with great clarity and I think some of these are worth recording. My state was, of course, one of extreme elation, the libido free at last to work out its salvation in terms of drawings. I drew incessantly and with this fantastic overflow of work came a changed mood. The pendulum was swinging both high and low, high as a kite where my work was concerned, low in my meetings with people. I experienced, for the first time, the inability to meet or talk with people, which I now know to be the first sign of depression. I could talk with my servant and took him into my confidence; we were somehow in this affair together. But I found it very difficult to make contact with anyone else, and really had no wish to. I was in a world of my own, blissful at the start, but as the feverish drawings con-

tinued it became a truly hellish one. Where I had drawn representational self-portraits and 'Singing Flowers', now came such
drawings as 'As I see myself', a fierce self-portrait expressing much
of my inward agony. It was an ambiguous drawing; it reflected
both my inward agony (uncertainty, perplexity in this seemingly
transcendental world, perhaps the darker side of mysticism), and
the confusion which results from a lack of comprehension of our
paradoxical and dual natures. Certainly at that time I had no
awareness or insight into my complex inner structure, although
the work which flowed so passionately from me expressed, in no
mean terms, this duality. Double meaning, dual imagery, extrapolation, the mystery of word-play, and my fierce paradoxical
nature, were to continue to play a vital part in the following years,
once more disastrously, because I had no awareness of myself as a
whole, or total, person. In that Greek room I sensed only, while
making this self-portrait, my sorrows, my humiliations and, more
important, the devil within me. I thought that by making this
drawing, I could, just as primitive man used to do, exorcise this
devil, which was fast closing in upon me and sharing my room.
Walt Whitman puts it so well when he says:

> "There was a child went forth every day,
>   And the first object he looked upon, that object he became,
>   And the object became part of him for the day, or a certain
>   part of the day,
>   Or for many years or stretching cycles of years,
>   The early lilacs, became part of this child . . ."

Alas, for me the 'early lilacs' had soon faded, and fierce reeds
had sprung up beneath my slippered feet; my mind became a
boiling pot of confused and terrifying symbols.

It is important to mention at this point that despite the hell that
was closing in on me, I was still ecstatic and receptive to mysterious messages. My whole state was receptive to words, gestures, lights, the smallest happenings. My awareness was accentuated to a fine degree. My powers of empathy, of projecting

myself into the objects around me, were fully ignited. I seemed to comprehend the soul of man, his joys and sorrows, his aspirations and failings, in the simple objects which surrounded me. As I have recorded, the washbowl, the paraffin fire, the joyous flowers, my dressing-gown, the flow of objects upon my desk, all these became a target for drawing and contemplation, and I understood (in a flash) much that had previously been denied to me. A second interesting aspect of empathy occurred during that day. A letter from my mother lay upon my desk. Its contents were just the usual gossip and good news from home, but in a flash, while inspecting the handwriting, I sensed drama and distress within the writer. It is true that I knew that all was not well between my parents, but I had had no definite news of their separation. The handwriting spoke to me, clearly and frighteningly, of deep emotion and danger. It is interesting that (although this was all subconscious) I burnt that letter along with many of the drawings, in an attempt, I think, to exorcise this source of danger, as I had tried to banish the devil by exposing him in my drawing.

Now, with many similar experiences upon which to draw (and which will be related in later chapters), I believe implicitly not only in the strange and powerful forces of empathy but in psychic connection between man and man. This strange and startling experience, which started in that cookhouse, opened up the path to a world of extrapolation, the calculation from known objects and experiences of a series of other terms which lie outside the range of the known ones.

I swept into another passionate hour of work. My dressing-gown was the source of a fresh batch of drawings. With fury I extracted the image of God, a serpentine, floating white shape growing from the circumscribing black lines. With God firmly translated on to paper, my confidence grew, and I drew 'boldness' itself, extracting the profile of a proud, naked man from the dressing-gown; within this was the hint of a woman devoured by the bold, masculine form.

My confidence began to wane and the next drawing was en-

2

titled 'Remorse and Pride=Determination.' There was still the strong hint of pride, of a torso bared to the world, but this drawing, with its hollowed construction, reflected the start of my inner uncertainty. The very wording was an attempt to justify the conflicting emotions battling within me.

Following this I drew 'humility', a headless, female nude leaning forward in humble supplication. From this gesture of humility, I moved into a series of drawings in which a naked woman seemed to be turning away from me and hiding her head in shame. This batch ended with a dramatic back view of this same naked woman, her hands firmly clasping her bowed head. Beneath it I wrote 'What's wrong?'

I started to quote passages from the Bible, inserting my own convictions as the words tumbled one upon the other. Some of these I poured on to paper, fiercely attempting to link the words with the drawings which had flowed from me. "That which was from the beginning, which we have heard, which we have seen with our own eyes, my own eyes, piercing points of demon light, which we have looked upon and our hands have handled, as a sculptor does in clay, of the word of life, OUT of the world of life; for the life was manifested, shown crystal clearly and I do bear witness, at this very minute, and declare unto you the life eternal which was with the Father, Son and Holy Ghost. That which we have seen and heard, I declare unto you, that you and I may rejoice, REJOICE I SAY, that we may rejoice and our joy be full. As the heart panteth after the fountains of water, so my soul panteth after thee, O God. O God I declare myself to thee, in all my nakedness, with a heart that only thou can purify, and my tears shall mingle with the salt of the earth and make rich the bread which rises from within it. My soul is troubled within myself, therefore will I remember thee from the land of Jordan, the mountains of Greece, the land of Thermopylae; and the hills shall rejoice in all the lands. I will love thee, O Lord my strength, my firmament, my fire. My trust is in thee, not in the law, *Dura Lex sed Lex* (the law is indeed most hard), but is it just? Just to the soul of man inspired by thee? Thou hast turned thy face to me, I have seen thine countenance not only in thine tabernacles but in those faces worn by woe. Why skip the lambs round the plains of Belsen, is this their nervous twitch for the sufferings of man? If I may dwell in your house, may the streams cease their panting and each child's hair be blessed in counting. Dear God, *Dura Lex sed Lex*, but made by man, surely not by thee? Preserve me O Lord, for I have put my trust in thee."

My whole being was electrified by some unknown source of current. Everything was linked and unified in the room, the fearful with the marvellous. I experienced a rare quivering pressure in my head and it swerved out through my arms into my hands and on to the paper. I was riding a bicycle down a steep hill, without brakes, and using no hands. Looking back on it now, and on other similar experiences, I realise that it was an attempt to fuse the negative and positive within me, to unite completely, which is one of the strongest psychological factors in our lives: the constant demand to unite, to be 'at one', to marry once and for all. Unison, yes that is the operative word which urged me on, endeavouring to fuse a previous image with the one before me, and inside me. For once real unison is made, life is a little less difficult.

Recently, during a time in hospital for further leg operations, I understood more clearly the duality of our natures, through a simple visual image, which expressed to me the strife within us between good and evil, our Jekyll and Hyde personalities, the link between anima and animus, our paradoxical make-up and our daily conflicts, when I watched a nurse using a pair of scales in the ward. I was a little drugged, lost a little to the world and its full realities, and lying relaxed upon my back. A nurse was having difficulty in measuring two quantities against each other on a scales. The left dish insisted upon outweighing the other, and I saw in it the bully in life, the one with the 'whip hand'; the right dish, uncomfortably aloft, seemed to stand small chance, as does the 'little man' in life, of exerting its influence. Then, quite suddenly, a small miracle occurred. The nurse equated the scales more nearly to a perfect balance, there was a tremor of delight as the two opposing dishes made a final frictional effort to disagree, and then there was perfection as the dual forces married in harmony. Even in my drowsy state, my heart stirred with joy at this revelation and perfection. And in the final tremors, before there was final marriage, I sensed the last moments of the love act, when animal fury and passion have abated and there is a stillness, a 'lostness to oneself', a union, which is entirely free of the ego. I thought that perhaps this greatest creative act of all possessed, in its way, the eternal instinct of man—the death wish; I thought, perhaps that is God's answer to our duality of nature, in whose action is found the safest way of 'dying to oneself', creatively and positively.

Soon it must have become apparent to my fellow officers that all was not well with me. During the night before I was finally hospitalised, I panicked, trying to gentle the pendulum, and burnt nearly all the drawings in my room. It must have been a dangerous action and the sight of the ashes in the morning was the final factor in my being put under observation.

I do remember one other rather special incident whilst I was still in my room. A very beautiful Greek girl, whom I knew well (she was an excellent pianist), came to visit me with a fellow officer. She might have come straight out of a Byzantine mosaic; she had large dark brown eyes and an almond-shaped face of great beauty and simplicity. Tanya brought me a small bunch of flowers; I remember their fragrance and perfection, their paleness against her olive skin. I seemed to know that she was coming and the flowers seemed a sort of present from God. I saw her as the Virgin Mary and imagined she understood what I said to her. I felt her to be part of the story, and as soon as she was gone I did, most reverently and calmly, a drawing of those flowers. I remember the hour of that drawing, and the immense peace it brought with it, and placing it by my bedside. It is interesting that this was one of the few drawings that I did not burn; I saved only about a dozen.

Soon an ambulance arrived and, without protest on my part, it drove me with my servant to hospital in Salonika. The world outside seemed very strange and bright, quite different from anything I had known before. Heaven seemed to be all around and I felt that no harm could befall me.

I remember my arrival in the hospital clearly. Once I was in the hospital I felt trapped. I desperately wanted to get out. My last visit to a hospital had been as a child of four when I had undergone a double mastoid operation. Suddenly all the memories of those painful weeks flooded back; the smells, the movements, the whole world of hospital life suffocated me.

The matron invited me to tea in her small office and it was a remotely frightening distance which separated us across the white-clothed tray. Her very kindness brought a certain fear to me; why no questions about my reason for being there, why such soft-spoken words and maternal comfort? I felt completely well, why this charade between two persons of such differing professions, she a nurse, me a young fit officer? The disjointed words which I heard myself utter were part of a dream; if only I could make just a few direct and sensible comments, on the weather, the china tea, or the flowers on the desk. An urgent need rose up in me to prove my health. But the very effort confused my mind, and each time I heard myself referring to my fatigue, it was in answer to a question of quite a different sort. How long had I been in Greece? Too long not to be tired, I said, and then realised that the question was not really a probing one but of social intent. Or was I wrong? Was this sweet-faced lady, in her cape and veil, cunningly probing into my secret life, prising me open with a refined and glistening tea-spoon? 'Another cup of tea, Mr. Rossiter, I always think a cup of tea the most refreshing drink of all?' 'No—no thank you so much—not another—you see I don't need refreshment of any sort.' I began to sweat. By denying that I needed refreshment of any sort I was giving the game away. Perhaps she guessed what I had meant. Did it matter? No, this was wrong, I must accept another cup of tea, to reassure her that I was quite normal. The rhythm of movement was halted in my arm as I passed forward the cup. Had she noticed this? If only I could relax and make a normal flowing movement. Then correct words would follow. Had she noticed the tremble of my hand, as I replaced the cup, and the small spill of tea into the saucer? No— I didn't live in London—no, I lived in Berkshire—that was, when I was there: I meant to stress that I was in Salonika, and that I knew it. Yes, Berkshire did seem far away—but I did not mind of course—I liked it in Salonika. Yes, the sun was hot—but that was not the reason for my dislike . . . no, I loved it here in Greece. I was trapped in my chair. What movement could I effect which would easily and gracefully take me across the room? Yes—I must go—it had been so kind of her. . . . I must stay? For how long must I remain? Oh, just for the night, well that could be arranged, I would ring my servant about the matter. He too was here? Fear closed in tight upon me. I lost contact with the room, the matron's voice, nothing existed except a spinning vacuous space, my voice a thousand years away, and I could not disguise the tears which trickled down my face as she gently took my arm.

I do not remember clearly the following few hours. The next scene is in a small ward and it is night. A nurse and an orderly are standing in the room. I am lying on a bed, my whole mind focused on escape. I am a prisoner to the ELAS troops. I am given some large white tablets. The tumbler of liquid held to my lips is some Grecian poison disguised as water. I spit out the tablets and swipe the tumbler to the floor. Swift as an arrow I spring from the bed, straight for the window. I am overpowered and bruised and hurt. Figures fill the room, all male ones now, they are sinister and tough. They pin me to the bed. A large clumsy sack is being wrapped around me. I struggle violently. Hands fiercely grip me, a blow is struck across my face. I can feel the slow trickle of sad blood running down my chin and warming for a moment a patch of neck. I struggle more. Violently I twist my body to resist the prison of the sack which is enveloping me. There is coarse laughter near at hand which incenses me to even greater effort. Another blow, straps girth-tightened all around me, only my head able to move, and again a blow across my face. The struggling which is outwardly controlled writhes within me; humiliation is bound tight into my soul. Trussed into this claustrophobic mass of cloth, I know the pain which far outweighs any other sort. I am a lump of despised goods, bundled up and thrown into the courtyard for ridicule, my frightened and bleeding face a symbol of my worth. The graveyards of Belsen close in upon me and I am at one with the scenes which were enacted there. Pills were forced down my throat; I vomited again and again as more pills were thrust into my mouth and shovelled down. Weakness began to creep over me; hazily I believed that if I were to sleep, I would die as a man does who slumbers in the snow. I opened my eyes wide and stared fiercely at the ceiling forcing the drowsiness out of my system, calling upon all the strength that I could muster. I must escape from these evil forces; and so, inch by inch, I loosened the binding jacket around me, biting into the rough cloth with my finger nails. Clawing the inside of my prison, I became a cat tearing its way out of a tied sack, hysterically working to free itself before it was dropped into a lake. Sweat poured from me, swamping body, arms and legs, slithering the confined movements; oiled surfaces turning moisture into fire. Flames sparked from my bloody finger nails searing into the tough canvas, as I singed its interior walls, and with one tremendous heave I burst forth from the tomb, past the dark figures, and leapt through the window. The crisp night air slapped my naked, sweating body, and it tingled as it had when my bare bottom was flogged by the birch at Eton. There I had been ground into an aged wooden block, my humiliation the greater for the force applied to hold me there. Then I had been freed to pull up my trousers, as now I was to scramble up from the soft welcoming damp earth and speed, swifter than lightning, into the dark, wide world of freedom. I felt as light as the air which hurtled past me. I was propelled by an inner driving force born in the claustrophobic confines of my recent prison, which fired me into the night glistening like a flaming arrow, hell bent on escape. I streaked on, flying over grass and paths and shrubs, divinely naked to the skies, and threw the whole force of my immense strength into the khaki figure standing in my line of flight. With all the resources of my army training, and much more, I hurtled at this sentry quietly dreaming of Blighty, girls and a pint of beer. I remember little more. I was knocked unconscious by my servant, who too had hurtled from a neighbouring window in pursuit. The full force of a midriff blow collapsed me in a crumpled heap; a broken, cold, dry-sweated lump of naked humanity, far removed from the world of heavenly visions and transcendental glories.

Those days and nights in that Salonikan hospital are an almost total blank. I know that it was there that I became desperately ill, with thrombosis in both legs and double pneumonia. The cold night air which had greeted my lithe and glistening body had turned those shimmering beads first to particles of ice and then to thawed congestion in two gasping lungs. Whilst I lay semiconscious, refusing stubbornly to eat or co-operate, three powers of sickness crept up on me, probing mind, chest and aching groin. There was a subconscious resistance to their powerful onslaught, a stubborn refusal to submit to an enemy that seemed to have all the resources upon their side. I fought with my subconscious mind, my distorted will turned to only one intent, to resist any further humiliations, to give not one more inch of ground away. A fight to the last ditch.

I faintly remember being lifted on a stretcher out over the water and lowered on to the deck of a ship by a crane. But my real memories of this part of the endless nightmare lie deep in the unconscious; sometimes these moments are stirred by some scene or movement or gesture, and for a second, I remember something of significance, but most of it is lost.

When I awoke in Athens, I was critically ill, both legs were useless, and my father was there. He was holding two tangerines.

CHAPTER THREE

FULL CONSCIOUSNESS DID not return immediately. I cannot say how long it took. I can only measure it in terms of sensations, scents, movements and sounds. I cannot even accurately place my father's appearance, with the two tangerines, amongst the misted jungle of those days. I must paint a picture glazed with shadows and half tones. There were no full ones. It was a world as remote as Limbo.

I remember certain voices. My father's beautiful voice remains vividly with me during some parts of that blank period. Not words, just the tonalities, its gentleness and reassuringness. The essence of it was love. But my memories of it, at that time, fluctuate. Some are obviously muddled with more conscious moments much later. I remember too the voice of the matron. Somehow I know it was her voice, not because we talked when I was more fully recovered, but through an inner sense which operated even during the darkest hours. Her voice came from far away, floating over my bed, and was absorbed into the wall behind me. She seems to be standing over me, and yet her words were remote and far away. Constantly this picture returns to me, a green woman, a green matron, a plump figure, hovering over my bed. I liked her voice, but I cannot say why. It was often with me. Never giving orders; just a voice.

My bed was on the floor during some period of this stage of illness. Of this I am sure. I see a terrible room with broken windows and low beds on all sides of me. Men are curled in blankets. Often they use their urinal bottles and not with full success. There is an incessant stink of urine. Brutal laughter invades the scene. Sometimes I am ill-treated. I remember bangs and bumps; did I fall off the low bed or a higher one? Perhaps I was moved to the lower one after this event. Certainly I bounced heavily to the floor on some occasion. I remember the bump which my head received. Rough blankets rather than sheets shrouded me. The thinness of my body is vividly with me. I could feel my bones at every point. I associated myself entirely with those terrifying corpses which the Allied armies came upon in the concentration camps of Europe.

The emaciation of my body, and the physical pain which pierced my legs and chest, were to me at that time a certain sign of my wickedness and desperate need of redemption. I felt that this was my penance, and that I must undergo all this suffering to redeem myself for twenty years of wickedness. And yet the more positive and sensible part of me struggled to keep alive, to win through, to beat this apparent enemy who was torturing me in this fashion.

The stench of stale tobacco holds a place in my memory; was it in that long, crowded, window-smashed room, inhabited by skeletons like myself? Did people really abuse me or is that my twisted memory? Bed changing: I do not remember my bed being changed down there, the changing of sheets was in another calmer more friendly place. I remember only coarse blankets, the rancid odour of stale sickness, and sweat-dried limbs. I was often carried somewhere.

I remember putting myself into trances by counting certain numbers. I perfected this system, when my eyes would disappear into my head, by the patterning of certain figures, and I would transcend time and space. I have distinct memories of this. It had a link, somewhere along the line, with significant numbers such as seven, nine and three. I do not remember much physical pain in that low slung bed . . .

There was one night of intense pain. I do not associate this with the 'basement room' (for that is how I picture my horrid resting-place). It may have been in Salonika, when I think I first contracted thrombosis in the left groin. But somehow I feel certain that it was in Athens, when the electric stab first fully pierced me. There was much movement around me. There were lights everywhere. I was seated in some form of tilted chair. I remember this clearly. But more distinct are my memories of kneading the pain out of my groins, massaging intensely with both hands deep into the furrows of the groins. Maybe others did it for me, but my recollection is of my own savage efforts, to swamp the pain and dislodge it from its source. It was a battle, it seemed of hours. My efforts drowned me in a flood of perspiration. Was I also at one point drenched by a bucket of water? I shall never know. I do not remember the operation. This was performed, I am told, to stem the clot from travelling to my heart. But I have no recollection of it. In fact I only discovered the scar in my left groin when being prepared nine years later for another operation, this time to aid circulation to the legs. 'Thrombosis Night'. This is how I think of it. Although it was a night of intense pain, and fevered attempts to stem it, it has a certain memory of glory. Perhaps it was 'all those lights' after the dank dark lower room, the tempo around me, the sense of fight and challenge. Memory is a strange thing. So much of it is clouded in discolorations, distorted by time and our subconscious needs. But that night for me did possess a certain 'Cup-Tie' atmosphere, no doubt induced by the incessant flow of movement around me and considerably aided by drugs, not so dissimilar in effect to drink. And I do remember being on the winning side. Somewhere, deep dark down, I have a picture of contentment and victory, of being, if not the victor, at least of the crowd that cheered the right team.

This victory is symbolised by the memory of clean sheets, lying very still, no more sweat, gentle movements around me and a shaded light. My stiff-ribbed body was as cool and calm and clean as the smooth, tightly drawn sheets upon which it rested. Intuitively I realised that the smallest movement would unbalance this calm procession, in which my fragile body was drifting into a dark tunnel, the 'cage' which raised the upper coverings above my legs. And so I drifted into that well curved arch by no effort of my own, high above the world of Athens.

Chronology, as I have mentioned, is impossible in recording those days. The scenes and sensations which I have described probably lasted over a period of a fortnight, perhaps a month. I have not checked dates with my father. He has reminded me of certain facts, such as the critical condition in which he found me; it was not necessary to have confirmation of my deteriorated state when first he saw me in that Athenian ward. His description of my total collapse, physical deformity and Belsen-like appearance only confirms what I remember, subconsciously, of those terrible days. I mentioned in the last chapter that I had faint memories of being lifted by crane on or off a ship, whilst lying on a stretcher. Whether this was in Salonika whilst being transferred to the larger hospital in Athens I shall never know; and it could not matter less. But what is of interest is a story which my father, usually a sceptic in such matters, told me a few years later when I was fully recovered. He told me that he had had a dream, a few days before the arrival of the War Office telegram stating my critical condition, and that in this dream he had seen me being lifted on some strange apparatus like a crane across some water. He awoke frightened and tense and then dismissed it 'as just a dream'. In fact, of course, I was being conveyed to the ship en route for Athens by just this means; and this, to me, is a significant example of synchronistic phenomena of the type which Jung explored so thoroughly.

Closely linked with this phantom period, of low beds, broken windows, remote voices and heavy bumps, are the experiences encountered on the journey by ship to Athens. Time again of course is irrelevant. The journey from Salonika to Athens is a short one. But in memory it was an infinite period of nightmare punctuated only by darkness. I use this word metaphorically, for what I now recall was experienced often in full consciousness. I suffered more severely on that journey than at any other period of my illness, mostly I am sure through my own imprudence and difficulty as a patient.

I have no memory of entering the ship, but I have a distinct picture of the cavernous belly in which my stretcher was placed. I seem to see a huge structural rib curving to the side of me. I am enclosed in a throbbing vacuum with two male medical orderlies to look after me. I am often difficult and refuse to lie down. There are memories of fights with the orderlies, blood, blows, more bleeding. I remember in particular the face of one of the orderlies; It was not a pleasant one. Perhaps I am doing him an injustice, for his was a difficult task, but I remember much cruelty, exceeding the necessary force needed to restrain me.

Sitting on a pot under the glare of the lights, almost naked, remains with me. Further fights; someone giving me a most painful spinal injection—I seem to remember two of these. Is it my imagination which links the look of sadistic satisfaction upon this orderly's face and this great pain? I remember the other orderly as kind and gentle and rather weak. It would not be truthful to say that time has healed completely the memory of that painful and terrible journey. A scab is left, an irremovable scar. Hate filled the belly of that ship and its wounds went deep. From these humiliations, and others that I experienced in my first year at Eton, I understand the full force of bullying and hatred. So that when I hear a Negro referred to as a 'bloody nigger', immediately I understand the incisive sword-thrust wound.

From the fierce hold of that ship I go to a period below the sea. This is scarcely a metaphor, for I had contracted double pneumonia and my subconscious world was swallowed up, it seemed, by an ocean of water. I struggled for a time beneath this sea, a submarine existence which has no real dimension in memory. I was probably immersed in an oxygen tent during that time and my laboured breathing effected the drowning sensation. Just a few images are still with me; I seem to be surfacing, coming up for breath. There is a ship with two funnels and two masts. Gramophone records eject themselves from the funnels and whizz between the masts. My parents' voices scream from them. Suddenly the deck is full of people. They begin throwing the records about, all over the decks; there are smashed remains littered everywhere.

I scrabble about on my knees searching amongst them. The scene fades, the screaming voices recede, only an occasional record flies through the air. I am no longer drowning. There are new sounds, heavy and consistent hammerings. (Later I learnt from my father that this was some roof repair being done above the ward.) The incessant banging continues, in memory, for a long time. Suddenly it ceases and I can breathe fully again. There is the scent of apples and grapes. My bedside locker is loaded with fruit. The apples remind me of Eden, the grapes of wine and the two tangerines of my father.

Success is a good feeling. Many of us strive after it in some way, right through our lives. When you are recovering from a severe illness, each day, often each hour, brings with it successes, and much of the struggle and pain is screened. You learn much with so many hours spent resting and just thinking.

I learnt first how to move with animal precision. I realised instinctively how critically ill I was. I did not hear a nurse say, 'Well, doctor, he's a gonner—he won't last the night,' and then suddenly become fired with enthusiasm for life, fighting back to prove my nurse wrong. Heroics of this sort happen only in films. When you are critically ill, you are aware of it, and the slender chances both ways. But being so ill, exhausted and with so few reserves left, you become animal and respond in an animal way, conserving energy intuitively, lying in just that position which will afford less breathing effort, moving with infinite care and precision to avoid waste of energy.

I would lie perhaps for three hours quite still, quietly considering how best I could move my position. A plan would form when I could mould my thoughts to a gentle movement which would entirely conform with the feebleness of my energies. Partly considered, partly intuitively, I would roll a few inches over, timing my movement in accord with my reserves, as a climber assesses and judges the next step of his ascent, so I would judge my movement. Having turned half to my side, and resting for breath, I would have to take the chance a climber does, for the next step. There was always risk in the next roll, which my weak mind could not imaginatively assess. A pause, sweat in the hands, sickness in the stomach, now I must take that chance, and further turn so that I was upon my side. I would count three—and roll. And there I was, entirely on my side, gasping for breath but still alive. The risk had been worthwhile and I had seized a chance, as a mountaineer grasps at a fingerhold, when I had clutched at the sheets tucked to the side. I lay exhausted, but happy in this progress, feeling almost fit again.

The return brought fresh thoughts and problems. How to move on to my back again, with so little energy still left? My mind would play about with rhythms, movements, jerks which would most speedily effect this end; but my courage quailed at the thought of testing them. I was a stranded survivor of some sea disaster, close to the safety of a bobbing raft. Some device, some prayer, could roll me from the cold outwastes of the sea on to the platform which would be a secure resting place. Again and again, I would stifle a half movement in fear. Had I the strength needed for this strenuous and athletic twist? I would realise then that only a two-fold action would assure this, a roll (that was easy) and then a jerk to put me on my back. I would count three, begin to roll, and then make a feeble jerk; and there I was upon the raft, flat on my back. The room, now sky around me, spun; I was drained of breath; but the glory of success swam in my head.

There was another matter, of bursting importance, which required more than animal precision, more skill than most animals employ on this essential task. I could not just select the right patch of earth, scratch away, perform my task and cover it again. The strangely tilted bottle would be passed to me discreetly under cover of a clean white cloth. A cold horror would fill my hands as they clasped this clearly obscene object to my bosom. Shuffling beneath my coverings (what a conspiracy it was), the grim act would begin. The nurse would discreetly leave the room. I knew from experience that my time was limited to five minutes. Six at the most. My system may have been aching for this conspiratorial chance for so long, but no sooner was the bottle in place than the sluice-gate would slam down, and only a trickle would filter through. A hint of warmth would spread into my fingers, but I longed for both my hands to be swelled by a miraculous flood of warmth, filling them with weighted pride, and the bottle full of golden liquid. Panting turned to the patter of feet—pause—the door flung open. 'Ready now?' Ready now! Yes, ready indeed for anything which would achieve the flow which both of us so impatiently required.

When at last the glass coffin, full of gold, was shrouded by the clean white cloth, I was entirely emptied of more than pride.

Lying on my back, with a cage over my legs, I saw the world from quite a different angle, both literally and metaphorically. The pendulum had returned to a more even rhythm, through sheer fatigue and illness. But as I increased in strength, so my mind took flight again, wandering here and there, in and out, round and about many subjects. Painting was never far from my thoughts; the last contact with the outside world had been through my pencils and drawing block. I started work again as soon as my fingers would hold a pencil and whilst still lying on my back. Mostly I drew my face in a small shaving mirror, using greasy chalks. I still have some of these drawings. Beneath them are scribbled such words as 'Slow Recovery', some date of importance at the time or significant comment. The words are mainly calm and objective, the drawings being a diary of my progress. The grisly one marked 'Sick in bed' is tilted on the paper, giving it the feeling which I experienced in this unaccustomed drawing position. I was no longer drawing essentially to release emotions, being far too weak physically and emotionally to attempt, or even want to do this. But I detect, looking at that drawing again the other day, a certain passion, considerably weakened and burnt out. 'Slow Recovery' is a strangely economical drawing, pipe in mouth, contented and calm. Another shows me from a foreshortened angle, slightly twisted; I must have been still flat on my back for that one. It is a strange drawing reflecting fairly objectively my twisted feelings. The drawings are fascinating to me because they are a brief diary of those difficult days, a personal record of my slow and painful recovery. I can truthfully say that I am not hypnotised by them because they are self-portraits. Nearly all of us are interested in our own faces. To admit this is not to confess to an obsession. It shows, besides possible vanity (which I think the least sinful of vices), a real and deep interest in matters which are important: character, age, the strain of life, experience, ugliness, beauty, elegance, wit, and the 'seven o'clock shadow'. Certainly, standing back in time, these drawings hold me for what they were and still are for me, as good an account of myself as I could give at that time.

I have no memory of the problems involved in making those drawings. I must have enjoyed doing them, for the number I did, but those first days of full consciousness are blurred by drugs and weakness.

A certain summer stillness surrounded those first delicate days of recovery. Drained of emotion, and often drugged into oblivion, I grazed peacefully in a calm green meadow. The rustle of a nurse's apron, close to the bed, reminded me of the gentle stirrings of fresh summer leaves. I longed to put out my hand and touch this virgin white, to be part of the gentle rustle and to bury myself in its cool embrace. My fragile thin body was echoed in the narrow white vertical apron pleats, pressed like myself almost to extinction; they tempted me to link my compression with theirs, calmly ascending the slim track, until together we met the contrasting blue belt, and married in the harshness of the glistening buckle. I recognised the severity of the almost shiny starched lower seam which flashed sharply against the black stockings; and when for a moment it touched my arm or body, it both kissed and cut me.

Whilst the nurse bent over my legs, making dressings, the

movement of her veil married itself to the movement of her head and I found new faces and expressions in every twist and turn. As a long-haired man nonchalantly flicks the forward strands back into place across his head, and changes in one swift movement disarray to order, so did the nurse turn one expression into another and disguise her mood. The sweet nun-like shape of face would in an instant turn to alarm, spiked by some new angle of the veil, and then even more quickly twist to pride as a shaft of white crisp linen swept swiftly upwards. I wished that I was part of the face which that sweeping veil enclosed, or a part of the watch which was so neatly pinned to the apron bib. I was filled with dismay as the watch fell vertically forward while the nurse bent over my legs, and delighted when it married itself to the bib as she stood up straight again.

Groups of objects, around the room, changed their aspects continuously. A humorous, light-as-a-canoe banana, joking with a proud apple, could change to a shifty, sneaking serpent who had just done Adam out of Eve, for a mere fiver, and was slipping off to find fresh gardens of delight.

When I took the small shaving mirror into my bed, I saw the image of a darkly brooding face, shagged in beard, with two black eyes bruised in hurt. The reflection of my suffering was etched into the deep shadows surrounding them, and I was immediately reminded of Rouault's portraits; my face shared the humiliations of his 'Ecce Homo', and graven into me were the lines which etched his 'Lex est Dura sed Lex' and his tragic clowns. I knew then the close link between tragedy and humour. Only a few weeks before I had been full of laughter. Now into the emaciated and lined face had crept sour juices which, in small beads, clustered in the caverns round my eyes.

The sheets had increasing appeal for me. Their whiteness suggested heavenly matters, and as they rumpled about me, I dived into seas, rode high on waves, and plunged into caverns on the shore. Lying in my bed I crossed vast rolling oceans, thrown from one white crest to another, and at times, rested for a while on some flat plain of ice. I could read anything I liked into these cascading forms, which turned from boisterous sea swell to a crisp white scapula within a second. The scene changing continuously, through glimpses of desert, dark caves, mighty swollen clouds, the bones of animals and men, back to the galaxy of a well inhabited sea-bed.

On top of the sheets lay the blankets; so great was the electricity in my body that the wool strands responded to it, and rivulets formed themselves in magnetic patterns across me almost instantly after being tidied. I watched these furrows form, fascinated. I could even 'order' my blankets. And if I passed a comb through my hair, it was done in one movement, so silky and waved were the formations. The voltage which I carried must have been considerable.

I became acutely aware of the space within objects. I entered, with a whirl, into the wastepaper basket close to my bed, spiralling down into the crumpled paper, dead flower heads and discarded wrappings. I crawled inch by inch over the anguished paper, frozen in death, staring pathetically up at me. I was reminded of the twisted and agonised figures in the Belsen camps; there was a link too with the creases which appeared on a nurse's apron.

I was almost able to converse with objects, the remnants in the basket, my bed rail, the sheets, the pillows, the ward radiator. Again I found them to be my only real contact with reality. I did not associate the radiator with heat or comfort; it was an abstract construction of great strength and simplicity. I remember calling it NOBILITY. The fine perpendicular lines of the pipes were as beautiful as a Gothic window; I gained as much delight from this radiator as I did from any conventionally beautiful object.

I think it true to say that during those two or three weeks, whilst I was still very ill, I lived a life of pure aestheticism. I was involved with everybody and everything on a purely aesthetic level. This is considerably easier from a hospital bed, tended by nurses and with no responsibilities other than turning over.

I was even being fed at the time. In my semi-conscious state, I had refused to take food from the male nurses. It nearly cost me my life. I was near to starvation point when my father arrived, sent for by the War Office because of my critical condition. Immediately he took responsibility for having female nurses moved into the ward (not really allowed in military psychiatric hospitals) and I began to respond again. This was only natural: I had regressed in my ill state to a form of childhood, possibly further back than I realise, and was demanding food from the sex that had first given it to me.

My recovery, physically, was gradual; I was in a divided world whilst I lay in that ward with the pale winter sunshine filtering through the blinds. At times I found it difficult to meet and talk with people, particularly difficult to make jokes; I was so riddled with guilt that easy conversation was impossible. I felt this guilt most acutely when I was being washed. Lying on the bed, with just a blanket covering me, my whole state of wickedness seemed to be exposed. Portion by portion of me would be bared and rubbed clean with a warm soapy flannel, the last part cooling before the next was attacked. The humiliation was reinforced by the cold bite of air on the recently cleaned part, which seemed to say, like a voice from childhood days, 'see what a naughty boy you are'. When finally my whole body could be dried at once, the rough warmth of the vigorous towel reinforced this message. 'See what a naughty and inconsiderate boy you are, wasting my time like this.'

When I was alone I prayed quietly to myself, sometimes for hours on end. Sometimes I found the unity and bliss about which, I think, Christ preached. I was individualised and yet in close unison with everything. My mind floated away from my body and reached out to the heavens. Visually everything was of importance. The pattern and relationship of objects was greatly heightened, just as it is in great art.

I have sometimes experienced this sensation whilst playing games. At a certain moment, with the rhythm and flow of a game 'just right', I have for a flash perceived this unity. The picture is seen as a whole even before it's started; the swift moment of decision on a football field, and its utter rightness, is known without thought and linked inevitably to other events over which one has no control. It is a moment of perfect unity. I am sure such perception was no rare occurrence with Stanley Matthews; you could sense it as you watched. I am not of course trying to link the marvellously healthy state of a great games player with the unbalanced state of a pendulum swinger. But the feeling of 'oneness', of everything suddenly unified and right without reckoning, this I am comparing. I am sure there is a fundamental and deep link here, where white-hot reactions and rhythms are essential for the perfection of a moment. 'A flash of imagination', so declare the daily papers when some fine athlete has achieved something unique. They are not wrong; inspiration is there. I find it interesting that the few pendulum-swingers whom I know have been fine games players at one time in their lives. And so it is with the pendulum. During the high fling, one seems to understand, for a short while, everything. Nothing is obscure. Light shines on the world, glowing from within you, and illumines everything. The truth is gloriously revealed.

I can explain this type of revelation in the following way; it encompasses almost any object or person by the vital perception which occurs during such a state. Consequently a newspaper heading, handwriting, a face, a gesture, the image of man contained in an ordinary object, marks on the road, and of course the natural scene, be it a townscape or landscape, all these speak to one with clarity and purpose. In a newspaper heading, I sensed in a flash, not only its total significance (which a good heading should do for anyone), but also in an uncanny and synchronistic fashion, the pattern and thought of the article below. I was already aware of its vital contents. With handwriting, my empathy towards the person who made those signs on paper is crystal clear and accurate, I think. And so with that most revealing of all 'objects', the human face. During such perceptive moments, it is possible (if I use with much self-discipline my rule of Look-ing, Listening and Learning) that I can read much about the per-son, just as a psychiatrist or great portrait painter does. A dazzling empathy, a mutual exchange, occurs between the two of us. It is a most powerful feeling and not far removed, I think, from the dynamic influence which a fine orator can impose upon his audience. Hence, morally, the necessity for its positive and good, use. A gesture, of course, to any perceptive person betrays much of the personality of its maker; this is well known to psychiatrists. It extends, in my case, to the objects which man fashions, a bowl, a pair of scissors, a painting or a stubbed-out cigarette.

Nature too, of course, unfolds its secrets to a perceptive eye, its vitality and certainty, its tough struggle, its endurance, its savagery, and other qualities which are needed for growth, sur-vival and decay. The objects which man combines with nature, inserts if you like, such as country gates, posts, road signs, walls, bear not only the image of their makers, but (and this is one of the subtlest combinations with which I am involved) they also record man's struggle to combat nature, to stem or prune it back; or to use it positively.

It is indeed a blissful experience whilst it lasts; alas, the opposite is true hell.

Lying in that Greek hospital bed, once the strong sedatives had really taken their effect and subdued the 'light', the world which I inhabited was indeed true hell. It became a world where the merest action, word or sight loaded me with guilt. The ward which had so recently been charged with magic and bright lit-upness (which had forced me at first to wear dark glasses) was changed to a rectangular space which pressed in on me from all its planes. The ceiling was a menacing flat surface which desired only to descend to the floor, crushing me to pulp upon the bed. It was a press kept from its active purpose only by the four walls, which themselves were inscribed with nightmare signs and scrawls. The notice pinned to the farthest wall was a four-line message of doom, neatly patterned to effect its meaning more clearly. There seemed no way to avoid the pressure of this pending press, unless I was to agree to the messages upon the supporting walls. Frantically I turned to reading their meaning; on each circumscribing plane some new warning was to be found. The windows were gaping rectangles of light, burning in upon me, and when shuttered against the Grecian winter sun, they became horizontal stripes fiercely flayed across my mind. The world was intent on first torturing me with keen biting whiplashes whose wounds would be salted by the white letters branded to the notice; and then finally, in an agony of pain and terror, I would be ground to extinction between the floor and ceiling.

I returned again to long hours of prayer and solitude. I lay like the stone effigy of a crusader knight, hands pressed together across my chest. I was in prayer against the walls which threatened me and which would soon entirely destroy me. I prayed for the strength to resist this pressure; I prayed too that if this pressure was brought to bear, at least I would have the courage not to cry out in pain. The grapes beside the bed would be changed to wine. I prayed that the blood within my veins would mingle with this wine and be the means of some delight.

I knew who was approaching my ward, and whether the door would open, by the tone and rhythm of the footsteps. A certain pace and slowing pattern filled me both with delight and shame. The door would open. My nurse, the pretty Welsh one, would appear. I would hang my head in shame, longing to look up; but I could not meet her eyes. How could I, this withered wreck, gaze up at that exquisite face, and hold my own? Urgently I required to lift my head and exchange a bold look with this pretty girl. But my head was seemingly weighted by a mill-stone, so that my beady, greedy, pin-point eyes fed hungrily on her lower shapes, which infested my whole being with even greater guilt. God!— how I longed to raise my head in full and glorious pride, to sing aloud, to love and praise, and to be accepted as a man by this perfect girl.

For a moment I did look up. My neck seemed to creak like a rusty hinge; for a second our four eyes met. Her beautiful pale blue eyes forced me to lower mine, snip snap, and there I was again anchored to abeyance, flooded in guilt. I had been tried, found guilty and condemned in one fleeting second; never again, I thought, would my head be raised in anything but shame.

Slowly I gained confidence, and with it the desire to draw more fully again. I longed to draw the willowy, exquisite young Welsh nurse, but never summed up the courage to ask her to pose. The request seemed indecent in my mind, when during the drawing I would strip her of her formality and her uniform. Often she would sit knitting in a chair close to my bed; I remember once she said, in a teasing Welsh tone, "When are you going to draw me?" I blushed and stammered some futile reply. But how my heart ached at that suggestive moment.

This stammering was part of my inarticulate self at that time. I could not communicate, except with my father, in anything but a 'sotto voce' tone, murmuring inaudible and disjointed words, which were stifled in my throat. My usual babble was reduced to tremulous hesitations as a result of my subconscious fear. There had been no brain damage, but a cerebral affection took place whereby my words were whispered huskily and with uncertainty. It is interesting, too, that when I did manage to speak with more assurance, my accent, and the content of my speech, followed closely that of two friends whom I much admired and who had influenced me a great deal whilst at Eton.

Christmas passed and I was gaining strength. My legs were badly swollen, white and entirely without feeling. I could not feel the nurse's hands when she touched them. As I lay in bed I suffered very little pain, just an occasional twinge or tingling. The pain was rather in the humiliation of having to have everything done for me and not being allowed out of bed. I remember clearly the bed-making, which is a skilful operation when the patient is unable to get out. I would twist myself over on to one side whilst the nurse drew out the sheet from beneath me. I would gaze over the edge of the bed down on to the floor, the scent of the sheets close to my nostrils. The mechanics behind me had an air of mystery and there was a sensual feeling to the whole act. Eventually, having twisted laboriously over to the other side (I was still very weak and easily exhausted), the bed would be completely renewed, and I would lie back on clean sheets ready for the day.

The day came at last, early in January, when I was told that I was to get out of bed, just for a few minutes, and sit in a chair, with my legs up. I manœuvred myself into the chair with the aid of two nurses and was suddenly shocked by the pain in both legs. Screaming needles seemed to be driving up them as soon as they moved from the security and padding of the bed. I was greatly alarmed and certain that the truth had been withheld from me and that I would never walk again. I sat back in the chair trying to hide the tears of shame and disappointment which were beginning to trickle down my face. The ward looked like another world, a world in which I had no part. It was perhaps one of the loneliest and most frightening moments of my life.

A few days later I was asked to put my legs down to the floor once more, just for a minute or so. So great was the pain that I cried out and withdrew them; it took some minutes to summon up the courage to lower them again and when I did I wondered how long I could bear it. I determined to stick it out for as long as possible, and only when overcome by dizziness did I retract them. I was convinced now that 'they' were fooling me, and that I was going to lose my legs; there was no chance of their recovery. Anyway what was thrombosis? I never remembered having heard the word before.

About a week later, with extreme pain each day when my legs were put down to the floor for a few minutes, I resolved a plan. Lying in bed with just the blue night-light, shaded by an old Monopoly board, I decided that I would make myself walk, by hook or by crook, alone while the night nurse was at her supper.

I hated the feeling of learning to walk again on the arm of a nurse, like the romantic posters outside the hospitals. This would be so much the final humiliation, in a period so full of them, that I did not dare to think about it. Only two months or so ago I had been dazzling about on a football field, and my entire youth had been spent playing games exceedingly well. I was one of the fortunate ones born to play most games well and with great enjoyment. So that my position, now, was a most humiliating one. But I determined to use my athletic prowess, my sense of rhythms, judgement of distances, my timing, to learn to walk again— unaided.

I bided my time. Soon the nurse would go to her supper and I would have half an hour to myself. As soon as she was out of the door, I leant over the bedside and threw my slippers over to the far end of the ward. I now had to get out of bed and retrieve them; my whole pride was at stake. I considered this struggle as a sort of game; I would bring to bear all my athletic senses on walking, somehow, to that far side, and then returning to the bed.

I lowered myself gingerly over the side. I waited for the singing pain in both legs to abate a little and then leant forward and gripped the bed table. I would use this as a walking stick and support. Slowly, oh so slowly, I shuffled across the room, the sweat pouring down my face. But I was still upright. Nearby was an apple. I let go of the table with my right hand and swept the apple to the floor, where it slowly rolled towards my slippers and then away into the other corner. The problem, now, was to get my slippers, put them on, and then, I was determined somehow to dribble the apple back to the bed. I would score a goal when the apple struck the urine bottle beneath it. Only then could I regain my lost confidence and be sure of the future. It was a grim struggle. At last I reached my slippers; quivering I put them on. I raised myself to my feet again and reached the apple. Slowly I dribbled the apple, inch by inch, to the beside and then, with a kick, the apple struck the bottle. It was a joyous sound, the ting of the half full bottle. No footballer has ever gained more happiness from a goal; I defy any player to contradict me. It was the greatest goal of my life, and the tingling pain in both legs became the vibrant roars of the cheering crowds.

Lying back in bed, my head swam with success, I noticed an egg lying on the locker, and without thinking I picked it up, determined to 'score a double'. If I could hit that night light, I was sure all my powers would soon return to me. I took aim and threw. Whizz! Bang went the light and the Monopoly board— darkness. My delight was immeasurable. Feet pattered down the corridor. The door flew open; I was scolded, there was a dreadful scene and the next day a psychiatrist was sent to see me. I explained what had happened. His long, sad face obviously did not understand; I could tell that he thought I had gone 'potty' again. Obviously he had never played games, never delighted in knocking a stump clear out of the ground or swerving a ball past the keeper. He made me promise I would never do such a thing again. I promised. But the yellow stain on the wall was my 'colours'; no cap I had ever won at school had meant so much to me. I was back in the rhythm of life; the fight was on and I would play tennis again, swim and slog a cricket ball about. The struggle, I knew, would be a stiff one, but if I could win this, then life's problems would never seem so large again. I had my target, and with this goal my ego-isolated world suddenly began to crumble; I found I could talk to people, laugh a little, draw things other than my face, read—and love again. Love began to surge up in me, love for many different things, from the basket so deliciously full of fruit to the radiator, and back to the temptingly slender black-stockinged legs of the Welsh nurse.

From that day onwards my recovery was accelerated and though I had still a long way to go, I never looked back into the utter depths of the previous weeks; if I was not in heaven yet, I certainly was not in hell.

Two things occurred in the next few days. I gained considerable confidence and I learned that my room had two separate identities: the one from my bed, the other from the chair in which I was wheeled away from the bed, for a half hour, each afternoon. In fact there was a third, and that was from the standing position; but as most of my time was spent either in bed or the wheel chair, the standing view was, at the time, one of less importance though very strange.

Although at that time I was allowed to stand only for short periods, I remember clearly the extraordinary sensation both of weightlessness (a sensation quite separated from my decreased physical weight) and, too, of the feeling of great height. As I stood for a moment, held secure by a nurse, I seemed to be taller than the mountain, with its snow-capped peak, which I could see from the window. I seemed to stretch into the heavens, far beyond that white peak, at first with a sense of power and pleasure, and then a few seconds later this sensation would turn to panic. I was somehow out of proportion with everything, the extended Alice-in-Wonderland of Lewis Carroll's story, and I longed for the potion which would restore me to a normal height, in line with the pretty nurse, my bedtable and the window ledge. But as I learnt to walk again, so it became less and less strange.

The pendulum went on swinging. The funny little wicker chair in the corner was alive with man-filled emotions, really rather a 'silly little chair' but trying, most courageously, to be otherwise. It almost succeeded. My blinds, Venetian ones, were stern and unbending. With their pale colour and strict horizontality, they bore little relationship to anything which I associated with Venice. The apples in the bowl were fantastic rubies, picked from some magnificent crown; the bananas, humorous, slightly sly and very sure of themselves. My father's tweed suit boasted rough friendliness and his wristwatch was a chip off some falling star. I watched these objects which filled my daily life with increasing joy; it was then that I knew I should make a complete recovery, however long and hard the struggle might be. I was 'in love' again; the 'one-ness' and glory of life was beginning to fill the room again. This glory almost dwarfed the numerous flowers which decorated the tables; it was something much deeper and fuller, something ecstatic and seemingly mystical. It was a direct link with God. God seemed everywhere, in apples, in the radiator, in the wicker chair, in the clean white linen sheets and the ever-swerving veils of the nurses.

In that Greek ward, with the pale January sunshine gently filtering through the blinds, I experienced both high and low, alternating each day. But I was down from the summit. There was snow on the mountain ranges but I was no longer treading its depths. The swings depended a great deal upon the recovery of my physical powers and how my legs were behaving themselves. I still found it difficult to communicate with anyone except those nursing me. I continued to stutter and lose confidence if a stranger entered the ward.

I remember that I was learning to walk, with the aid of crutches, and feeling much better, really rather joyous. I was leaning on crutches, peering through the slits in the blinds, when the door opened and my father appeared with a friend. I remember my inward collapse at the sight of this second person, the sweat in the palms of my hands and the dizziness in my head. It was as if a vast ocean separated us; my father and the friend were standing far away on the other side. My father was clearer to me than the second person, whose form faded at the edges and blurred with the objects in the room. Speech was impossible. I tried to say something and move at the same time. Nothing happened. Neither did my legs respond nor my voice utter. Slowly my father helped me to a chair. Seated in this my voice returned, but I heard strange and stutter-distorted words emerge from within me. I do not remember much more about that visit, when my world, for half an hour, again collapsed. I remember the loneliness which I experienced when they had left, the feeling of isolation and lack of contact. With the entry of a brisk nurse to aid me back to bed, something of the more stable and confident world returned. Here was something which I understood, definite orders, the hospital routine, the decisive and effective movements of the nurse. It was a link with the only world of security which I understood at that time. The uniform was a symbol of security and understanding; probably it remained in my subconscious memory from mastoid days, as a boy of four, when I was dependent upon nurses for recovery and confidence.

The next few hours were filled with recurring doubts and confusions. In that brief visit much of my newly won confidence had been shattered. But resting back in bed the scene slowly changed again. Amid the doubts and confusions emerged some of the confidence won in the past few days. From my bed I recognized the world which I understood and had begun to accept as a pattern. The discipline of my life, during that period, depended upon my position in relation to the room and the objects within it. From my bed I knew exactly where everything was and should be. The very order and tidiness which surrounded me was my security. As soon as I emerged from the bed, to sit in a chair or walk a few paces, my security was lost. It would return, if I was seated for long enough, in some measure; inwardly I pined for the one place in the room from which I could 'command my affairs'. Out of bed, the fine perpendicular lines of the radiator were no longer an echo of my dream desires, of stability and perfection; rather they became upright shapes, swollen by unevenly painted surfaces, to which I would totter for physical support and guidance. As I clung to these pipes, my hands aware of their imperfections, so my dream world faded into the painted scars and nobbles. I would stagger to the flat smooth enticement of the bed table, only to discover that this too had imperfections, and a hint of damp upon it. My grappling hands, longing for the cool embrace of a smooth and unquestioning surface, would touch something which belonged to a world from which I had retreated; and when my fingers paddled in a hint of water, undetected from the bed, I shrunk back from a world so charged with mess. Even the window, so calm and rectangular from the bed, was scarred with scratches and omens of life with which I had not reckoned. The ledge itself, beneath the half-open, tempting window, was soiled by marks which for the moment had no place in my retracted world. The room which had so recently been a perfect place, digested and fully understood, had become a room of three dimensions, one of which was too closely linked with the world I feared. Man had inscribed this third dimension with an ugly meaning, and I wanted only to know a world translated flat, on two plain surfaces. As I clutched the bright red apple, lying so complacently amongst its friends, I became aware of all the sins and temptations which the world outside possessed. Hurriedly I withdrew my grasp, wiping my hands clean of the hint of grease, and stumbled back to bed.

Lying back in bed, with some of my confidence and spirit returned, was a good feeling. I could breath evenly again. There was a gentle knock upon the door. It opened, and there stood my father, in that rather too long and most friendly check overcoat. I can never see a hint of this country tweed pattern without a feeling of affection. He stood by the door for a moment and then moved towards the bed. "Hello, boy," he said, "I forgot to bring you these books this afternoon." He paused by the bed and with that tentative and unforthcoming movement, stripped of rhythm, which often disguises deep emotional feeling, he placed two books upon the bed. It was as if he had given me something with which he did not wish to part. Instinctively I knew what it was. It was a strangely moving moment. It seemed to say, 'I know what happened this afternoon, sorry, m'boy, here's something to make up for it.' I was aware during those few seconds of all the profound and deeply sensitive qualities which my father possesses, and which are disguised, to the outside world, by a soldierly, white-moustached appearance. Those rare and special qualities flowed out to me, during that moment, in abundance. It was not a moment of sentimentality but rather one of profound senti- ment. My father is very English in his distrust of outward emo- tion. It is from my mother that I inherit a Latin feeling of out- ward emotive expression.

My father sat down on a chair away from the bed. It was as if he had committed too much of himself at the first moment of entry, and now must retreat to restore the balance. A gap in space and feeling came between us, only to be unified by the tears which welled up from deep down inside me and ran uncontrollably down my cheeks. The blur brought us together again, my father's coat rippled unevenly at the edges and its brownness merged into the dark linoleum on the floor. His hands however remained distinct; I remember them gripping the chair and moving it forward nearer to the bed.

My father had brought with him two books, both of which were to play an important part in my life. One of these I knew well and had loved since schooldays. This was *The Memoirs of a Foxhunting Man* by Siegfried Sassoon. The other recently published, was called *Brensham Village* by John Moore, who first established, I believe, his reputation as a writer about country life with that book. It would be impossible for me, ever, to evaluate Moore's book objectively. In that ward, Moore brought the scents, sights and delights of English country life right to my bedside. I owe much to both these writers for bringing me back to the world, back from absurd Olympian-fancied heights to the real joys of country living. My decision to work and live in the country was considerably influenced by those two books.

The books brought the English countryside, the ditches and hedgerows, the downs and hills, the ever-changing light, right back into my life. At that time the picture was heavily over-sentimentalised. I still wept easily. A certain pattern of words, or a, particular phrase, would quite unexpectedly bring tears to my eyes. Through them I pictured a rose-covered cottage 'somewhere in England', with sheep grazing nearby in a field. I wept, most, when the words brought vividly to mind the delight of fresh grass, blossoming orchards, autumn evenings and rich ploughed fields. I saw the dark cuts of earth as fat slices from some vast Christmas pudding, lying diagonally relaxed across each other. And immediately my mind would turn to neat rows of stacked roof-tiles, and my father's building activities. Tears would dribble down my face, blurring the words upon the page, as a ripple fade-out does on a film screen. In place of the images would be Victorian sub-titles such as 'The Doctor's Choice', 'End of a Perfect Day' or 'The Last Letter'. The end of a perfect day for me, in imagination at that time, were two young country lovers holding hands across a gate. I longed passionately for real and perfect love like that, all of a scented evening, the only barrier an easily unlatched white wooden gate.

I felt myself to be a beaten chess piece, lifted from the board and discarded into the dungeon of the box. Lying in bed, I imagined only the two dimensional pattern of the world outside; from my slanted position, in bed, even a chess board was changed from menacing squares of black and white to less finite shapes and contours. My mind chased patterns as sunlight seeks out a zebra's stripes.

I was painting by moonlight, the backs of the sheep Palmer-illumined in light. Cows were stilled in their fields, Dutch-engraved upon the scene. The roses were scented with the fragrance of paradise. Corn stood head high, golden and supreme. The torment of Van Gogh's meeting with corn was lost to me, in that idealised hospital state, whilst I hungrily devoured the calm and measured world of Sassoon. That was to be my world, for ever and ever. Quite forgotten, in fact not comprehended at all at that time, was that an artist's meeting with nature is fraught with danger. I only saw the egg-shell blue sky and the occasional cotton-wool clouds which drifted dreamily across. The world I imagined had not even the briskly invigorating clouds of Constable, and the soft earth which I trod was dew soaked, not drenched by torrential storms.

In the ward those two books were constantly by my bedside, replacing the fierce imagery of the passionate artists with whom I had first surrounded myself.

I had encircled my bed with books from the library, and my

3

own collection, upon whose contents I could feed hungrily. I found in these prints the approval of my powerfully sensual delight, and my eyes could delight in their form and drama. It was immediately apparent to me that my interest in these paintings lay, fundamentally, in quite a different field from my interest in the pretty young Welsh nurse. That latter interest filled me with guilt and confusion. I saw myself as the 'dirty old man' of Shaftesbury Avenue who pawed and pinched unsuspecting girls. But when my passionate delight swooped upon a Rouault, a Matisse, or an exquisitely sensuous Modigliani nude, my mind was filled with no inhibition or jot of guilt. Pride welled up in me, intellectual pride I suppose, that I could love and understand these paintings, which so much puzzled my three nurses. When any one of them leaned over the bed and glanced at the glowing forms and colours, immediately there was a gap between us. The importance of the nurse's work would recede and in its place was something impossible to value. These books, and all they meant to me, somehow, during the time they were my companions, drove a wedge between the nurses and myself. They were out of their depth. I longed to lecture them for hours on the exquisitely sensitive, ever-travelling line of Modigliani, a sculptured line which travelled as smoothly and crisply as a railway line, intent upon its purpose. I saw the link between the tired jacket of a peasant boy, and the worn dress appearing just above the apron bib, which a nurse wore during a late evening session. I longed to marry those patches, so tactilely the same, and thus bless the nurse in art.

But there was a wide gulf between my love for these works of art and the vacant look on the nurse's face, who bending embarrassingly over my shoulder, would exclaim, "Well, it takes all sorts to make a world. But if I looked like that—well, I'd die." I hated her for this, for her crass and insensitive ignorance, and for a short time relegated her to the rank of a kitchen maid.

I found a close connection between the white virgin areas of apron which the nurses wore and the white costumes worn by

Soutine's cooks. I began to talk widely and wildly about such matters, and about the delight which I found in Rouault's dark brooding faces which so reflected mine.

My father had removed these art books, quietly and without fuss (so he tells me now), a few days after giving me the two English books. I do remember a sudden feeling one morning, on awakening to find the art books gone, of being cheated. 'They' were doing things to me again. But I made no protest; I had not the will or courage to make a scene about anything. I felt myself to have been deprived of all rights and dignities, an eternal sinner.

I certainly remember those two country-praising books as being the starting point to brighter days, to less prayer and solitude, and gained strength. To add that I dozed off to sleep with one of those books clutched in my hands would be a Victorianly sentimental way of stating their importance to my recovery. The scene may well have taken place, for that is the essence which lingers with me when recalling those first 'real' days of recovery. Contentment. A goal at last. A link with the Berkshire Downs and my home, and with the scent of the rich ploughed earth. Even Sister's brisk and businesslike voice, saying, "It's time for the bed-pan", could not contaminate the freshness of the dreams which now filled the ward.

Bedpans play an important and uncomfortable part in the lives of all who are confined to bed. It is as if they were designed, not only for humiliation, but for some task other than the very natural and necessary one for which they are intended. My chief memory is their genius for sloping backwards suddenly, or forwards, just when one felt security. And is it just distorted memory which makes me remember all the bedpans which 'aided' me as too small? Perhaps we had the less well-designed ones shipped out to us. At one time my bedpan had been, however trivial, my throne. From it I gave orders, my courtiers clicked to attention and scurried off. Now that normality was returning to my world, the 'morning seat' was merely an uncomfortable and much disliked part of the day's procedure, something with which I longed to dispense.

Recovery was a sure fact now. Each day saw real progress on one front or the other. Increasing strength, regaining the use of my legs, feeding myself, lighting my own cigarette, all these things, and many more, brought immense joy. I remember the particular fragrance of my first cigarette; it possessed a magic, far-away, scent; for a moment I recaptured that first 'fag' behind the haystack of boyhood days. I remember doing my first jig-saw puzzle and being able to control my hands sufficiently to fit the pieces together. That was a great moment. And of course it was marvellous to be able to draw again and not lose myself in a world beyond my comprehension. The hallucinations had disappeared and my mind was beginning to work normally again.

The last few weeks in that Greek ward were essentially happy ones; gone was the dark hell of a month before. I still found it difficult to meet people, but this is only a comparative matter. I am essentially gregarious, so that the change to finding difficulty in meeting people was more marked for me than it would be for a less gregarious person.

Late in January 1947, I heard that plans were being made to fly me back to England. My joy was great. I could not walk very well yet; just sufficiently to move around. The sun, shining pale as a primrose in the ward, reflected my delight. In generous fashion I offered my arm for an injection; this I was told was to help me sleep on the journey. The ward was suddenly stripped of meaning. As the nurse rolled up her sleeves, I sensed the same gestural significance which is expressed by the hotel porter who rolls up his sleeves, bends down, lifts the packed suitcases and strips a hotel bedroom of a fortnight's stay.

I became a part of the evacuated luggage while being lifted on to the waiting stretcher. For a moment I sensed something more than merely being part of the leaver's luggage. I felt that the room was being cleared, almost in a rush, of all its ugly memories.

Only my withdrawal from the room could give it a chance to air, to breathe again, to be just 'room fourteen'. I wondered how many weeks or months it would take the room to return to its noncommittal, boring air. I found a certain urgency in the way in which the stretcher was carried from the room, as if a plague victim were hurriedly being moved elsewhere.

Suddenly, after a long hollow passage journey punctuated by rectangular windows and strange unaccustomed shadows, I was tipped legs downwards. I felt right through my body the firmer grip upon the stretcher handles. It seemed to say, "We'll bloody get you out of here, if it kills us". A cockney voice just said, "Steady, sonny, hold on, it's the stairs". Fierce needles rushed into my legs. I dared not cry out in pain. "Steady, sonny" had been a humiliating phrase. I desperately wanted to prove that I was a noble, courageous, battle-scarred young officer, who knew 'how to take it'.

The sun smote me with a shock between the eyes. I felt that all my thoughts and feelings must be X-rayed to the world by this fierce exposure of light. Where I had just been another part of the pattern formed by the primrose light within the ward, I was now a blatant, bright yellow dandelion, ready to be mown down by the engines which I heard nearby.

My father was waiting for me. I saw his brown checked suit and highly polished shoes dark against the concrete glow of the forecourt outside. A deep flow of affection swam between us. I longed to leap from the stretcher and shelter in his familiar shape, shadowed and enclosed from the brutal stare of the outside world. It was a world of immensity and light, and I was just a thin, dark X-ray plate.

In the aeroplane we all wore cardboard boxes round our necks, with our lunches packed in them. I was strapped to a stretcher which was itself strapped to the ceiling of the plane. I had been heavily drugged and only remember part of the journey. But I do recall the cavernous shape of the plane and the incredible cold as we neared England; for as many will remember, January '47 was an exceptionally cold month. I remember being fed my lunch, counting the screws above my head, exchanging glances with my father, and the discomfort of lying for so long on the stretcher with the increasing cold. But it is a hazy recollection, as also our landing, when my father left me to return home.

I suppose it had never occurred to me that I should not be going straight home. Certainly it came as a bitter blow. I was by myself, for the first time in weeks, in the sick bay of some aerodrome in the South of England. Snow lay deep around. The barrack ward was glowing white with the intense reflections from outside. My own reflection in the mirror looked dark and satanic; I was unshaven and very frightened. Again my memory of this part of the journey is rather hazy. I remember shaving and tidying myself up. I remember a rather unpleasant aircraftsman. I remember being taken into an ambulance the next day, and the crunch of snow. I did not know where I was going, but being tired and much in need of a permanent resting-place I did not question the nurse. I somehow accepted that they would take me to the right place, where I could recover fully. By now I had accepted the fact that I was not fit to return home, much as I wanted to. I had partially regained my trust.

The journey was a terrible one. In the bitter cold of that freezing winter, with the roads iced and snowed up, we trundled and skidded along, for what seemed days. In fact it was the best part of a day. The pain increased in my legs; I wondered if I could bear it much longer. Fatigue overcame me, I slept fitfully, longing for this appalling drive to end.

Eventually we arrived at a military hospital in Aldershot where I was transported by stretcher to a waiting room. It was a great relief to be out of the joggling and skidding ambulance, in a room that was partially heated. I was left for some considerable time, without even an offer of a cup of tea; my senses were numbed and I was near to tears. I just longed for the moment when they would wheel me to a ward and allow me to rest in bed. After about an hour a nurse appeared and I could hear people speaking from the doorway behind me. The nurse took my temperature; there was more talking. Then I felt myself being wheeled backwards, out of the door and into the open again. The nurse who had taken my temperature was beside me, wearing a cape; I asked her where they were taking me. She told me that I had been brought to the wrong hospital. I was lifted back into the ambulance and we started up again on a journey I like to forget. Much of it was hidden from me by my almost fainting condition. I was utterly exhausted.

It has always seemed strange to me that I was forced to undergo that dreadful journey just because I was a psychiatric case. The hospital in Aldershot was for 'ordinary' cases. I learnt as much from the ambulance attendants. That a person who had been so critically ill, and was only just recovering, both in mind and body, should not be allowed to rest for a night in an ordinary hospital shows the out-datedness of psychiatric treatment in those days, only sixteen years ago. It expressed perfectly the approach to psychiatric disorders of the past decade. It was an antediluvian state of affairs. Since then very great progress has been made on all fronts in psychiatric treatment. Meanwhile, I was to find an out-dated hospital near Southampton, built facing the wrong way. According to legend it had been muddled with a hospital planned for India in the late nineteenth century, and India boasted the one intended for the South of England. It was a strange and rather ominous place, not exactly planned to cheer up depressed patients.

I was fortunate to be looked after by a kind and wise woman doctor who soon put me into a cheerful ward. I spent my time at Netley learning to live again, learning to walk properly, to face people and master my emotions. I had little help from the hospital other than deep-ray treatment for my still badly swollen legs. My therapy was really left in my own hands and I realised that the way back to the normal rhythms of life was to play games again. Consequently I set about playing table-tennis to regain my speed of mind and reactions. I had to learn to run again; whether this was due to my breakdown or the state of the thrombosed legs I shall never know, but I found it quite impossible for a few weeks to run; I just could not make the necessary motions, a strange and frightening experience. I was a marionette whose guiding strings had become entangled, and my movements possessed the same stutter, or dislocation, which my voice had suffered in that Greek hospital ward.

Three of us formed a close friendship. One was a much decorated young officer who had had a nervous breakdown, the other a potential professional cricketer. I think we cured each other. We played cricket in the garden, table tennis in the evenings and cards late at night. We learnt to laugh again and to flirt with the nurses. I was still desperately shy of women, but it was good to be with two people who did not share this shyness. Between us we represented a whole, each contributing what the other lacked.

Our real cure came when we were allowed out into the town. Away from the hospital no one was to know our case histories and deep troubles. Southampton was very badly bombed during the war. We strolled the battered streets, went to cinemas, and drank endless cups of coffee in Tudor cafés. But there was one particular café which we inhabited each evening, a small working-class one near the ferry. It was not just that we got delicious buttered toast, tea, cream buns, vast plates of eggs, bacon, sausages and chips; there was a much more real, basic, and human reason. The proprietor's daughter, who served us, was a 'scorcher'; I really think she was one of the prettiest girls I have ever seen. We sat around our table pretending to converse about our futures, but our minds were far away. In her black, very tight dress and little white apron and cuffs, she had us panting with delight, tongues hanging out. We all longed to date her. None of us had the courage. Her name was Betty.

Then one evening after about a month, Jack said to me (he was the cricketer): "I'll bet you a quid you won't ask Betty to join us at the cinema". He felt his money was fairly safe. I thought the matter over for at least a week; I was still frightened of talking to girls, particularly very pretty ones. Even Sister, who was very good-looking, had me fumbling for words.

Quite suddenly the sun shone one splendid evening. The water, at the ferry crossing, glinted miraculously, the white posts stood triumphantly upright near the water's edge. There was a hint of spring in the air; it was late March. You could sense the sap rising in the trees, bursting to break out. Life was returning. And there was Betty, coming down the road towards us. Without thinking I stopped, saluted (how pompous this seems now) and said: "Hello, Betty—would you care to join us for supper?". She smiled her sweet smile and said, "Sorry, boys, I'm just off on holiday— but thanks all the same".

I had just won the hospital table tennis tournament and had nearly dated my first girl since being ill. I was more than a pound richer. I was well again, ready to take up the struggles of life once more. As we continued down the street my stick vibrated with joy. I twirled it Chaplinesquely in the air. In a few weeks I would be an art student. Life, indeed, was good again.

CHAPTER FOUR

I LEFT HOSPITAL on March the twenty-ninth and returned home. It was my twenty-first birthday. By a strange arrangement of fate this date coincided with the one on which I returned home after mastoid operations sixteen years before. There were several factors in common between those two home-comings. Both times I had been critically ill and then journeyed home, almost recovered, on my birthday. As my father drove the car through the gate leading to our cottage on the Berkshire downs, I suddenly experienced a tumultuous feeling. It was not the pendulum; I was still too shaken by my illness to experience high pendulum swings. It was a deeply emotive feeling in which the scents and sights, missed so long, flooded back, welled up inside and choked me. Tears trickled down my cheeks as the car drew to a standstill; I turned away from my father and fiddled with the suitcases, embarrassed by this unexpected moment of emotion. As I stood in front of the house, the March day became suddenly flooded in images, scenes of days decorated by ponies and picnics; and memories of eternal summer afternoons linked themselves to the recent experiences in Greece and all I had been through. But they were peremptory pictures which flashed through my mind, none of them lingering with me for close examination. For a moment I experienced the emptiness and disappointment which a much-longed-for return so often brings. The actual moment is so vastly different from its expectation. Although my mind was full of potentially evocative memories, of childhood and the recent past, none of them lingered long enough to be printed. My tears had been sentimental ones. I experienced little feeling during those first few minutes of my return; it was a world standing at a distance from me, brightly illumined by the sunshine, but not within me. I felt neither joy nor sorrow. I was held in a vacuum. Everything seemed to be happening around me rather than to me. The occasional snapshot which did allow itself to be printed was brown and faded, the world of Cairo, Alexandria and Athens as remote as those seen in photograph albums. In fact it seemed impossible, here on the Berkshire Downs, that those places could possibly exist. Something propped up against the front door brought me back into focus. It was a sack full of saw-dust. My kitbag, crammed full of possessions and capped with a tin helmet, printed itself fully on my mind. But kitbags, tin hats, mess tins and camouflage nets were things of the past. The saw-dust spilling impertinently from the sack was a homely reminder of my father's passion for building and carpentry. It was a link with something which I understood. I was back on the gravel drive which my father had been laying when I set out, so young and fit, so brimful of life, for the Middle East a year before. It was a strange and moving moment, that link with home again, full of subtleties which now elude me. The sack and myself so fully packed with old chippings.

But I do remember the particular scent of the garden, the young hedgerow which had grown two inches, and the feel of the plain wooden door. I touched it to reassure myself. I could scarcely believe that I was really home, away from the nightmare months which had encircled me during illness. Everything seemed strangely still. It was the stillness which says, "Yes, I'm here, but *you've* got to find me, probe me, I'm not unfolding to you". I realised then that the first move was mine, if I was to re-enter the world I loved, but which for the present was no part of me. It was the meeting of two lovers who have been parted for a long time; they have embraced different experiences, away from each other, and the fusion of these findings cannot be made at the first meet-ing. It is a sad moment. There seemed to be no link, except per-haps in a remembered gesture, a type of smile, the colour of hair. Gradually, over the days and weeks, there is a marriage, the gap is closed, there is a sharing again. But it is never quite the same, though continually in life we pretend it is.

I was home with a month in which to rest before becoming an art student. The month which senses the first glowings of spring, not the full burst of blossom glory but the days which shoot sap fiercely in the trees and spurt bulbs through the soft earth so that they may, a month later, stand shoulder to shoulder like guardsmen. It is the month of re-birth, for fresh ideas, new resolutions— and for getting well again. I had the full force of the Berkshire countryside working on my behalf, not pleading with me to forget the past, but signalling to something that could not be missed. Each flaming branch and peeping bulb was a symbol of something far greater than itself; it was the mystic sign of MUST, inevitable, true and perfect.

But I was still weak and without confidence. I could walk only with the aid of a stick and I trembled when anyone spoke to me. Tears were never far behind my eyelids and welled up without warning. Somehow the struggle in hospital, tucked away in the south of England, had been easier. We had been of a oneness, had shared each others' burdens. We had the community spirit so often sought by people in need of confidence. We were sheltered, able to heal in our own time without prying eyes. I had re-taught myself to play table tennis and catch a cricket ball with no one to laugh and despise my antics. Now, alone at home, I felt the isolation which is one of the most difficult hurdles an ex-patient encounteres.

The pendulum was almost still, sometimes drifting one way or the other, moved by a passing breeze. It was too tired to swing fully in either direction; it just longed to be left alone, to die and rust way. I could see the magic of spring and on occasion sense it for one fleeting moment; but I had no confidence, nor the freedom, to shout aloud those fine words of Robert Frost's, "Spring is the mischief in me". I had no notion to 'do mischief'; guilt still hung around my neck like a Mayor's chain, each ornament embellished with some darkened picture of the past. I felt dark and crude and ugly, face to face with spring. I could not erase the memories of my fragile body, at times without control, which had dirtied sheets and poured urine, sweat and tears into my coverings, I felt that I had sullied everything by these emotive actions, which had brought me to the level most animals would shun. The bright sunlight picking out a group of daffodils, spotlighting them from the others, seemed a symbol of God's Grace. I shared the loneliness of the ones not illumined by the magic sun; I longed for the warm welcome overflowing into the lit daffodils. And when the sun did strike my face, it was a searchlight piercing from a turret tower of some concentration camp.

At the apex of my chain of guilt hung a larger medallion uninscribed, but which would bear my future actions. I dared not inscribe anything upon it, fear gripped me, just as the sweaty palm of my hand gripped the ash walking-stick; fear of the world, people and the future. There was no laughter within me; I was hollow, scraped clean, my body a vacuous space. I would look intently into the palms of my hands, when alone down by the woods, and try to count the glistening beads. Were there more than yesterday? The handle of my stick, stained by these beads and my fierce possession upon it, became linked with me, not merely as my friend and aid in walking, but in sorrow. When the ash stick was propped in the hall stand, it became divorced from me, grimy at the handle, proud and resentful, scorning me for thus infecting it.

On the evening of my return there was a small twenty-first birthday party. As I entered the room I felt that I was taking part in a doll's tea party, and that none of it was real. Certainly the decorated sandwiches and cakes did not seem for me. When I allowed myself to acknowledge that these preparations were for me, I was filled with fear. Here on the tables lay exquisite patterns of food, their pretty sweetness accentuating the clumsy ugly sense within me. The small white candles seemed so very sure of themselves, like young bridesmaids at a fashionable wedding. The whole scene was absurd, some bizarre charade, a subtle mockery through neat triangular brown sandwiches, plates of delicately sliced meat and prim square chocolate-covered cakes. Their order, their refined insistence, their 'don't I look good', embarrassed me. They were as self-conscious as gnomes eternally fishing in a suburban garden. The sofas and surrounding chairs seemed arrayed to witness some sinister ritual act, whose real significance was camouflaged by the decorative display, like garlanded maidens encircled by vast Druidic stones.

I do not remember much of the party with clarity, for such was my fear of meeting people that I lay on the sofa isolated and withdrawn. Some of it remains in my memory; my twin brother's speech, delightfully witty and unpompous. He thanked my parents for everything that they had given us in twenty-one years, everything except our most uncomfortable beds; he spoke for both of us and I was filled with envy at his ease and confidence.

I remember the beauty and gentleness of Rosamond Lehmann; while talking with her I sensed that she knew much that I had been through and I did not resent this. But her elegance and beauty increased my feeling of ugliness and inadequacy, and it was with relief that I was left alone on the sofa, to wipe the palms of my hands covertly when no one was looking.

I was an outsider to that party, and never once really entered into it. When the candles were lit they seemed a mockery; I was no part of this festive glow.

As I sat on my bed undressing after the party, I looked again at the silver cigarette case which my parents had given me. It was deliciously new, slim and perfect. I opened it. As yet no ochre twists of tobacco had wedged themselves into the corners. I opened and closed it a few times. The neat incisive clicks gave me confidence. For a moment I possessed the same assurance that a film hero does, handling such a prop. Fumbling in my excitement, I loaded a packet of cigarettes into the case. I closed it. The click was less hollow, more confident. I repeated it. My confidence grew. I withdrew a cigarette, firmly closed the case—paused—and tapped upon it. No girl would be able to resist me in the future.

Time had come to a standstill. The particular momentum of
hospital, the rhythm of ward life, had been replaced by the pattern of everyday family life. Instead of Guardsmen-lined beds and
tables there were the seemingly infinite plains of the Berkshire
downs. Gazing from a hill above them, they appeared as countless squares and rectangles, like sienna-stained pocket handker-
chiefs and lengths of scarves stretched out to dry in the sun. They
reminded me of the harmony of nature's colour, but also, more
horrifyingly at that time, of the innumerable decisions which
were mine, and only mine, to make. They were symbols of all
the patterns I might choose to make in my own life. I could
plough my field this way or that. I felt helpless to choose the right
course. It was more a matter of choosing any path at all. The fields
were patterned so correctly, their unity made possible by just
that stretch of green in relation to that rectangle of brown. It
was as if God had been directing the several farmers from above.
While they ploughed away, on tractor level, He had ordered the
huge canvas, as a film director unifies a complex and moving
scene. The final composition was perfect; nothing could be added
or subtracted without damaging the whole.

While I was ill in Greece, at one point, God had become a large
phoenix-like bird in my mind, and the cawing of the crows had,
only a month ago, spoken messages to me. They spoke to me,
personally, calling me by name, instructing me to do this or that.
But I was never silly enough to obey them—or too 'far gone'.
"O.K., you silly old buzzards", I would say to myself, "go on
squawking, screech away, you don't worry me." But of course
they had for a time.

Now I was past this state of hearing human intonations in
birds; I had heard words, too, on the wireless, addressed to me;
but now the wireless rarely mentioned my name, perhaps just
briefly, on an unimportant programme, late at night when I was
very tired.

Sitting on a gate above the downs I watched a hawk, caught
in the March sunlight, hovering. I wondered again if perhaps God

were some marvellous bird. That hawk perhaps? That noble, magnificent, regal creature hovering over the spring downlands. I was not alone in linking this species of bird with 'super-existence'. The Americans and Germans had hoisted his royal cousin, the eagle, to such a state, and Caesar before them too. The hawk, the more modest country-cousin—was *he* God? Did he hover over the fields while farmers ploughed their furrows, ordering this pattern here and that section there? The swift swoop and death, was that the visual manifestation of God's other face, like sudden death in a car crash, or corrosive cancer?

I looked up into the sky; it was egg-shell blue, perfectly domed, the hawk a minute dark tone against it, entirely still. I climbed down from the gate and as my feet touched the springy earth, my heart was suddenly filled with love again, filled to overflowing, the sky a world cathedral dome, the hedgerows my guardian companions, the sparkling grass a soft carpet for my swollen legs. The hawk was no longer a supernatural beast but a handsome British bird intent upon its search, which gave great pleasure in its flight. Who was I to quarrel with such an act? Did we give equal delight in return for our acts of cruelty? Did we humans, with centuries of civilisation behind us, compensate by such beauty for our terrible acts, our swoopings, whoopings and slaughter? Only three years before, from that very gate, I had watched a thousand gliders ride out into the dawn on track for the Invasion. Part of me understood that this act, our onslaught upon our enemies, had been a necessary one, to conquer a tyranny. But part of me was, and still is, horrified by such acts of wide and terrible massacre; I understood, because of my recent experiences, that man suffers enough from his own stupidity, and at his own hands, without the aid of others. As I stood on those Berkshire downs, I was filled with compassion for all those who had suffered, on all sides, in the last war, and prayed that such conflict should never occur again.

On that particular sunny afternoon I felt the first stirrings of love again. Standing close to the gate from which I had just descended, I noticed the worn nobility of its stance, the ochre sienna scars which it carried like medals for its years of service. It too had seen war and struggle, peace and calm. The gate was strong and wise, it seemed, on that sunlit illumined day. There was no conceit in its stance, only the dignity of a fine old Berkshire farmer, well weathered, worn and country-wise.

I picked up my stick and hobbled down the hill; my heart was lined with primroses, spring-watered, and buttercup-reflected.

During the time spent recuperating at home I was often filled with recurring doubts and confusions. One part of me regarded the past experiences as 'God-given', another part was suspicious and uncertain. It is only with absolute certainty, and objectively, that I can now quote a remark of the composer Stravinsky, who wrote recently: "I regard my talent as God-given and I pray to him daily for the strength to use it. When I discovered that I had been made the custodian of this gift, in my earliest childhood, I pledged myself to God to be worthy of it, but I have received uncovenanted mercies all my life. The custodian has too often kept faith on his own all-too-worldly terms".

At home I tried not to link my 'religious' thoughts with my desire to paint. My family steered me off this way of thinking, discerning the confusion this pattern of thought had brought to me. There was wisdom in their advice, most necessary at the time, but they did not comprehend the profounder matters involved. I was already aware of 'something beyond art', the link between the symbols of art and mystical matters, but was quite untutored in its usage. I had been given a sign, had only partially comprehended it, and finally betrayed it. Now, with one further 'test' behind me (where I also failed), I realise more clearly the link between the poor symbols which we use in art, and the mystic signs which are God's alone. That there is a link is now a certainty with me.

On the Berkshire Downs I set about the task of repairing my damaged legs; I managed to get them back into reasonable shape by walking, bicycling and playing tennis, pumping the circulation round them again. The pain was offset by the return of increasing confidence. Each day saw some improvement on both fronts. The memories of those four weeks are jumbled and are mainly not of interest to this story.

I remember many joyous afternoons spent with my sister Gilly, and Sally, Rosamond Lehmann's exquisitely beautiful daughter, at Wittenham, close to where Paul Nash created many of his mushroom-shaped images. Sally, perhaps the loveliest young girl I ever knew, with her long fair hair, contrasted perfectly with the dark and vital prettiness of my petite sister. They were between them the epitome of youthful beauty. We walked often in the fields around Wittenham, clambering over gates, and then would return exhausted and lie in deck chairs in the garden, Paul Nash's hill watching us dreamily from nearby. The serenity of those clumps, the freshness of the grass, Gilly and Sally and the immeasurable beauty of Rosamond, remain vividly with me and played a very special part in my recovery. It is easy to sentimentalise memories of this sort; at that time I was unsure of myself, and the halcyon quality which I found, recently, in some photographs taken then, is not the essence of these particular days, at least not wholly.

But I do remember, with much affection, the warm and serrated laugh of Sal's brother Hugo, while he investigated a newly discovered wooden bridge. It was one matter to play and fool around a wooden bridge; another to cross it. For so high were our spirits that often our enjoyment lay in obstructing the passage of each other for as long as we could. My enjoyment was as great as any during those games. But on the journey home some of the laughter would be left behind mingling with the mossed and worn wood. I saw the bridge then as no longer a friendly lichened stream-crossing, but rather a vast construction of iron girders, stretched overhead away into the darkness like some disturbing fantasy of Salvador Dali. Beneath my feet were wooden boards, spaced three feet apart, black and slimy. One false step and that was it.

I realised well that I had not yet 'crossed' my bridge. The breathing space at home was merely a bridge in time, not space. My test was to come, and the sweat rose in the palms of my hands when I thought about the next move. This was to journey to London, find digs, and start at the art school. Part of me longed for this new life, this fresh start. Part of me believed that the new world of art school and student life would obliterate my recent memories. But the most insistent part of me said, "You can't do it, give yourself just a little more rest, just this first term. Dash it, you've only been out of hospital a month". And there was just a teeny little flame, barely perceptible, which demanded notice, the almost extinguished flame of challenge and ambition. It is a power constantly with me, which thrives on defeat. The igniting forces of spring working their wonders all around me caught this flame unawares, and there I was driving up to London with my mother, clutching my gold-peaked Guard's hat to bolster the hollow pit within my stomach.

CHAPTER FIVE

MY MOTHER HELPED me find digs in the home of artist friends, in a charming house just off the Brompton Road. I was given a small room on the top floor. My glowing hat, on the washstand, symbolised clearly the difference between two worlds, the one in the near past, the other which I was about to enter. Some part of me, defensively, clung to the glamorous hat, the other real part demanded acceptance at the art school as a serious student and not as a dilettante.

London was bursting into spring, mischief was all around me, but still I had no share in it. That first term was a difficult one. I was still very shy, unsure of myself, and I stammered. Besides this, I had only my army uniform (I was not demobilised yet) and a pair of riding breeches. So that my appearance alternated between a potentially dashing young Guards toff and a young dark-haired edition of Munnings. The looks which I received did nothing to increase my confidence and I suspect that even my stammer was assumed to be a 'social status symbol'. I longed to be accepted; for here at last in the long narrow locker-filled corridor, nicely stained in paint, was the world I understood and loved. The studios overawed me when filled with students, who all appeared far more talented than I was, sure of themselves, knowing where they were heading. I longed to possess their nonchalance, their easy ways in the canteen and their laughter. Those first few weeks were truly unhappy ones. I felt isolated, unwanted and incompetent. Probably to an outsider I appeared brash and pushing. This was merely a disguise to hide my unsureness.

I liked to potter about the empty studios, which reflected my sadness to perfection. It was almost an act of masochism. In those large rooms, so suddenly stripped of their vitality and use, I found another form of loneliness which I could add to my own. It was a backward search, which might have gone on much longer had it not been for an incident in my second term. The first had been a disastrous failure. Only Rosamond Lehmann's encouragement had persuaded me to rejoin the school in the summer term. Just one incident restored my confidence and led to the world of freedom and laughter, and even more important, acceptance as a serious student.

I had submitted a painting of a street in Benôdet, done during the holidays in Britanny, to the annual sketch club. I remember joining the rest of the school for the 'crit' which was to be given by the Principal, Harold Williamson, in the gymasium where the works were hung. I wedged myself into the back of the hall as inconspicuously as possible. The Principal talked for some minutes and finished his introduction by saying that there were five paintings which he particularly liked, for entirely different reasons. He talked about four of them and then quite suddenly mentioned mine as the fifth, and as prizewinner. He explained for some minutes why he found my painting interesting, where its faults lay and what pleased him about it. I was flushed with excitement. Nothing will ever obliterate the memory of the joyous swing which my pendulum took during those few minutes. The room danced around me and the pictures became blurred rectangles of pure colour and delight. The faces around me dissolved into dots and dashes and the Principal became a thin perpendicular streak silhouetted against a blurred host of coloured rectangles. I remember only hazily leaving the hall afterwards and the many congratulations from unknown students. That moment was my ticket into the art school as a serious student. I have of course a most affectionate regard for that painting and have always refused to sell it. It now hangs in the hall of my father's house, not because it is a very good painting, but because its success meant so much to me at that time.

From that moment onwards I was back in the world of reality, laughter and light. It led to four years of much happiness, in which I squandered my talents in the usual boisterous ways peculiar to students. I learnt much but could have learnt much more.

I remember my world, at the start of art school, as still divided. Part of me was immersed in the bohemian pleasures of student life, part of me still clung to the upper-middle-class security of my parents' world. My mother's flat, sophisticated and ordered, contrasted strongly with the rooms and houses of my student friends. Lacking full security myself, often I found myself retreating to her world of Adam fireplaces. But I was aware that in these surroundings, so free of creative problems, lay a trap. I had no wish to touch and handle the well arranged objects in my mother's flat; I merely wanted their security and approval. Paradoxically my behaviour, when I did visit this flat, was often aggressive and out of tune with the surroundings. For the real and tactile artist in me pined for a room where created things grew. Despite the squalor of many of my friends' rooms, I found in them the quality which was most needed by me at that time.

Soon I moved into a world which was nicely situated between the two. A large and handsome studio, close to the art school, was owned by one of the senior students. Felicity welcomed me into her fascinating circle of friends, and to a room which I loved from the first moment I saw it. Here, in Felicity's Glebe Place studio, where art was synonymous with breathing I met a host of interesting people. Looking back over the years, I see a studio full of dearly loved books, pictures and objects, arranged with rare judgement, creating an eternally peaceful world. It was a world poised somewhere between Tissot and Bonnard. Here I first experienced 'itchy' fingers, and the passionate desire to live in such a room myself. So I collected round me objects which were close cousins to those in Glebe Place, and decorated my own first real home, a two-room unfurnished flat in Oakley Gardens. This studio flat arranged itself in much the same pattern as my Greek room in the Mess in Salonika, only now there were no hints of army business, just two rooms filled with the things I loved best.

Settled in my new studio, many of the past sensations surfaced again. I began to draw with some of the passioned fury of Salonikan days, unleashing rhythms and ideas which hammered continuously for release. At art school it was not possible to work in this abandoned way. I was ashamed to draw in this fiery impetuous manner. Guilt still lay within me, and subconsciously I connected this emotional way of drawing with sin, and ultimately with collapse and total darkness. I would look at the few remaining drawings from Greek days, realise the cost, and resolve not to express myself in this way again. It was probably wise at the time. My mind still needed rest and could not afford a torrent of ideas to flood it. Even now I have to ration my painting, for I know there is a danger point which can only lead to the uncontrolled swing of the pendulum. I work these days with more caution than I would have guessed possible a few years ago, at full tilt for a while, but with a keen ear for the shrill scream of the pendulum.

Not that I feared a return of my illness; that did not occur to me. The very name of the illness, manic-depression, had not once been mentioned to me. I heard mention of the word schizophrenia, hushed somewhere during my illness. But once I was free of hospitals, my illness was immediately relegated to the 'breakdown file', certainly by my family, and consequently by myself. Therefore I was not aware of what had really 'possessed' me, not did I sense any dangers for the future. I had had a bad breakdown, My father, I think, realised some of the potentials which might lead to a further illness. Often he has tried to persuade me not to get bogged down in the pattern of thought and reading which interests me most, and which he thought led to my troubles in Greece. But of course, despite the well-meaning intent of his advice, I have never, for long, been able to accept it. For my life and creative work are bound up with these matters, matters that I do not fully comprehend, but which I realise to be of profound importance. His kindly and fatherly advice was born of a real desire to save me from any future troubles of this sort. But I do not think, despite his immense sensibilities, that he has ever realised quite what happens to me when I am confronted by a Rembrandt portrait, a foaming orchard or a stream of objects swerving across my desk.

But at Chelsea, I played safe with that part of my life which was fraught with danger. This was mainly a subconscious reaction, not one born of considered thought. And 'Spring had such mischief in me' that much of my time was spent in explosive student rags. But there were times when the pendulum did swing more fully. I remember my first meeting with Soutine. Purposely I say with Soutine, rather than with his painting, for at first glance I met a kindred spirit who had done in his painting what I most wished to do. Looking at his magnificent crimson-cassocked, white-surpliced, standing choirboy, I rose with him in prayer right into the gaping heavens. There was in Soutine's work the ecstasy and anguish which I understood so well. I hungrily purchased a book on this master of deeply emotional poetic painting. He showed clearly the close link which ecstasy possesses with anguish; without reading his biography I knew the torments he must have suffered, and the heights he must have reached. I realised fully the reason for his death, at an early age, of ulceration, barnacles born of spiritual passions exceeding the endurances of man. These paintings fired me to work again.

I took wing on many an occasion into the visionary clouds and blossoms of Samuel Palmer. And I met Bomberg in full force at the Redfern Gallery. At that time he was mostly neglected; it is only in recent years that the London art world has woken to his vital powers. But I remember well my admiration and respect for his work, which cast an even gloomier spell upon the already misted ambiguities of the Euston school, who reigned triumphant during the late forties. I felt anger at his neglect and could not comprehend a world of art which put faded post-Sickertian niceties before those of a vitally compulsive painter who at his best spoke with eloquence. I was in those days entirely biased by my emotions. I can now see the subtlety and quiet magic of many of the Euston school, but still I am horrified at the neglect of certain painters. It is no wonder to me that it needed America to stem the flood of neo-Sickertian-umbered pictures which adorned most London galleries during my student days.

I was engaged on many fronts during those years, but none was more important to me than the search for paintings that spoke to me. Chardin spoke of perfection, peace and mysticism; Kandinsky of vital rhythms and a divine ecstasy; of the ecstasy and anguish I knew so well. Van Gogh and Kokoschka spelt the full force and vitality of man, though Kokoschka's force never burnt as deeply into my mind as Van Gogh's; this great Dutch-born painter meant for me certainty and positivity, and compassionate perception. And the poetic three words, Piero della Francesca, whispered a magic, mystic stillness which man has rarely equalled in the field of painting.

I realise now, after many years involved with paintings, that I never see the literary content of a picture at the first glance. It is the abstract essence which strikes me, and it is by this quality that I judge it. Slowly the realism dawns upon me, but the true 'reality' for me always lies in the abstract content.

I had not analysed this 'inner understanding' of a painting during student days. But I do remember, in recollection, that I was deeply thrilled by the baroquely voluptuous masterpiece of Rubens, 'The Rape of the Sabines', at the National Gallery, and yet until my third meeting with it had no real awareness of its subject matter. I thought of it as a joyously sensuous mass of movement; later I saw the infinite subtleties of the flesh painting; but it was some years before the words of my composition tutor at Chelsea, the distinguished painter Robert Medley, who referred to the 'mystical worldliness and delight' of Rubens really fell into place. During those student years, it was the 'glow' which remained most clearly in my mind: but perhaps I was nearer to comprehending Medley's remark than I realised.

I mention this, at this juncture, because it is vitally important to the problem of the pendulum. Objects, during the 'imprisoned' world of the Grecian days, had taken on another form; I had become part of them, comprehending their abstract content—by which I mean their non-occupational task. In that cookhouse I had first sensed the peace and exactitude of Chardin's world, in cups and saucers. Later, as I have recorded, many objects became linked to me in more fiery challenge. And so it was with paintings. And that is why I accept and enjoy so much of abstract painting, although I am myself what is called, for want of a better name, a representational painter. To judge a painting by its realistic content is to miss the point of art. That the details and story within a picture add to it, I do not deny, if they are sublimated to the original abstract conception. Any work of art of distinction is first and foremost abstract. That I did not fully comprehend this during my student days is not surprising; but within me I held the intuitive understanding of this important matter.

The years can easily glaze the past in nostalgic memories. I have no nostalgia at all for my student days. I could write of Renoiresque summer outings on the Thames, when students and staff mixed cricket with beer. Or of the 'Stunt', the end of the Christmas Term variety show, which the students staged, and which meant so much to me at the time. Or of the film called 'The Lost Chord' which I made with a handful of other students on the Berkshire Downs. But none of these events really looms large in my memory and certainly had no profound effect upon the pendulum. The joys experienced in these various activities were normal and fully happy ones, but without intensity.

But there was some intensity in my feelings for the autumn and winter evenings which are an inseparable part of the magic of London, if one loves that city at all. My memories of those foggy evenings, with the lights faintly peering through them, are deeply poignant, and are linked to childhood memories of pre-war London and the muffin man. This peculiar magic of fog and blurred silence, shapes rising mysteriously out of nowhere, smothered sounds and irridescent ochre stains around the lamps, was perfecty caught by Victor Pasmore in his romantic, and breathlessly still, paintings of London in the forties. If my description sounds sentimental, then I have made my point. A foggy London evening is charged with a special mystery and must arouse deep sentiment in anyone who loves London, and in retrospect this special sentiment becomes inevitably sentimental. Through my lace curtains (yes, I really had them) half appeared a timeless world, a world which demanded no ecstatic emotional advances, and yet stirred me deeply. I remember, too, exquisitely misty afternoons in Kensington, browsing round Jenny's fascinating antique shop, Jenny being Felicity's step-mother, and much linked with my happiest memories of art school days.

The self-indulgent, monastic world of art school passed and I had no regrets as I brushed down the visitors to the public lavatory at the Festival Gardens, during the last summer vacation. I enjoyed immensely that temporary job and gained some of the best tips on dogs and horses that I have ever had, besides the usual ones accorded to such a post.

When the vacation was over I went out to teach. I could not find myself a post in an art school, much to my disappointment, but took up one in the West Country in a small public school. I had determined to live in the country once I had finished studying, for I was more than anything interested in landscape. Also, my legs were ulcering badly and I knew that the country would afford me a more restful time, the queueing for buses and trains being a continuous strain on my health during student years.

I found, near Taunton, a small public school which might have come straight out of the *Bumper Boys' Annual*. But my heart leapt with joy to be deeply in the country once more and I sensed, at first meeting, that Somerset had something very special to offer me. I took a deep breath and, autumn filled in splendour, set about my task of organising the Art Department.

I remember many scenes from that happy term. But only one or two are relevant to this story. I recall with great joy a scene in a dormitory. A master, short in stature but with a huge moustache, and puffing an even vaster pipe, is on 'dorm duty'. A tall boy comes up to this little Napoleon and, towering above him, puffs at the infernal clouds of smoke. The master staggers back, unbelieving. "How dare you—how DARE YOU . . . blow away . . . blow away—my smoke." My pendulum, in sheer delight, responded strongly to that moment of supreme pomposity and I barely concealed my laughter. Perhaps that incident encouraged my ambition to get out of schoolmastering, and fired me with even more zeal for my creative work.

The world of dog-eared books, mortar boards, tired desks, and crisply functional matrons did beckon. It possessed calm permanence, upon which you could rest and rust away, very easily. But in its midst there were sudden glimpses of other matters. The blackboard streaked with signs and symbols which faced one entering a classroom: a master had left something more than just a white algebraic equation chalked upon a board, some essential and vital part of him was inscribed upon that flat dark enigmatic surface. And the pendulum leapt a little at those newly discovered and disturbing signs; the writing was, if not literally upon the wall, at any rate upon the board.

And in that remote negative world of quadrangles and equations, silver cups and gowns, fired by the full enjoyment in my task of teaching, infected with the golden glow of autumn, my mind chalk-streaked by fluent signs and symbols, I tackled with football fury my first white canvasses since leaving art school. I worked long hours into the night, in my small attic studio, covering vast canvasses which almost exploded from the room.

Many 'indoor fireworks' were produced during that term of work, none more important, to my career as a whole, than the vast backcloth for the end of term school play. This I stretched

across the bottom of the swimming pool—needless to say the
pool was empty—and into it I plunged, a figure brimful of
energy and gusto, waving a score of six-inch paintbrushes to left
and right. I danced over the vast canvas, my feet marks marrying
in delight with the sprayed streaks of flickering paint. It was a
'passion-pooled painting' which burst forth upon that white-
primed hessian cloth, created as the backcloth for a lyrical
Shakespeare play. I remember it clearly for two main reasons.
First for the great chunks which flaked off it whenever one of the
actors stamped too firmly upon the stage. And secondly for the
delicious scars it left upon the concrete bottom of the swimming
bath.

But more important, to my story, are the scars which that
activity left upon my aching legs. It was a foolhardy act to work
for such long hours, on that concrete base, with legs already ulcering so fiercely. No sooner was term finished and I had returned
to London, than my temperature rose. The ulcers had gone septic.
My mother gave me hospitality at her flat and there I started a
batch of fierce drawings whilst confined to bed. I drew mostly
my sheets and pillows, desperately trying to drag from them some
message of comfort. The anguish at once again being confined to
bed, just when life had seemed so brimful of hope, burst forth
from me and I scrawled a hundred signs and symbols on drawing
paper, expressing my state of mind. My bed sheets became high,
voluptuously sensual seas, the pillows defiant rocks, and objects
around the room were stranded voyagers cringing from the
wreck. And so I drew, with the impassioned force of Grecian
days, until my mind whirled into the same pools, which beckoned
my drowning state. My mind began to boil again, once confined
to bed, so that I lived much of that time in a world of images,
signs and symbols which were scored into the subconscious by
white-hot needles. For a short time I experienced that 'separation
from the body' so relevant to this state, where the outside and
practical world does not exist. But I was reminded of it by the

visits of my friends and the pattern of my mother's life around me.

I shall be writing more fully in the next chapter of many events, directly linked with the vicious swinging of the pendulum, during 'confinements', periods of enforced hospital treatment for my legs. I purposely use the word 'confinement', for a person of my vitality, exuberance and wide interests, experiences just this pregnant state when cooped up in bed. Ideas and images generate to profusion in this physically static state, and the urge to give birth to them shares some of the same pains as actual childbirth. And the pendulum swings with desperate force at times.

My removal to hospital for further treatment, and the first of several operations to aid the circulation in my legs, early in the New Year, affected me in several ways. Much of my anguish was assuaged by the quiet rhythm of the medical ward in which first I rested, before being moved to the surgical one. The drawings of that period reflect that calm and order. The pain, too, kept my spirits from too high a flight. And as in other long periods in hospital, I read widely. Those three months were a university term of learning. My companions, most far iller than myself, and the staff, were in a way my tutors, for I learnt from and through them many of the wisdoms which few university dons can impart.

I have often said, and how I mean it, that it's an ill wind that blows nobody no good. All experience is of value, if we allow it to be. But I had not that wisdom during my first sojourn at Queen Mary's Hospital, Roehampton. Much of me was bitter, self-pitying and childish. I felt myself to be back in square one, the black rectangle.

CHAPTER SIX

THE THREE-WHEELED, AIR-COOLED 1926 Morgan which valiantly carried John Brooke and myself through France, over the Simplon Pass, down into Domodossola and then on to Venice, via Lake Garda, and almost back to Ostend, in the summer of 1952, symbolises well my advance again from square one. I was once more in the world of student adventure. My lungs were filled with Alpine air and my belly with beer. And the dramatic end to this journey, when we hurtled at seventy miles an hour into the backside of a Belgian fire engine (and a cow), marks the end of my student wanderings.

The next four years, from Christmas 1952 to Christmas 1956, were perhaps my most importantly formative ones, when my life was fully occupied on many fronts, in particular teaching, painting, writing, running a taxi, and receiving further hospital treatment for my legs. Needless to say, I dissipated my talents and energies in a host of other ways, some of which are best forgotten. From these four fully-loaded years I shall select some of the scenes and events which remain with me most vividly and which reflect the changing motions of the pendulum. It was not an easy period for many reasons; in particular I had two thorns in my flesh—the inability to find a teaching post in an art school and the constant pain, and periods of hospital treatment for my legs, which interfered with my painting. I had not at that time learnt to live with my disability. Obviously, over four years one experiences much that is not joyous, but I can truthfully say that this period, when I made my first real attempt to 'broaden out', was a happy one. It was a time bursting with potentialities; some I seized, others I lost. But the sum total of those first real steps in the outside world remains with me as a very happy one. That I was neither cut out to be a schoolmaster, a teacher to handicapped children, nor a taxi-driver for that matter, is beside the point; I entered for a while all those worlds, and some others, with keen interest, enjoyed them a great deal, and learnt much from them.

The pendulum during those four years was sent swinging by a wide variety of sights, scents and events, but never, I cannot think why, to an uncontrollable point. So many memories that rocked it come to mind, while I am writing, that it is difficult to select the most significant. The ones which I record must represent a thousand similar ones.

First and foremost was the Berkshire countryside. Again I felt the compelling forces of nature beckoning me, and as soon as teaching was finished for the day, I would ride out on my bicycle to meet the gesticulating winter elms and draw the bristling hedgerows.

My real search into nature and the countryside began whilst teaching at St. Andrew's School, close to Pangbourne, the small Berkshire town which was punctuated, during term time, by three-quarter size images of naval officers. I began to probe fiercely into nature, often late into the evening, until I could see my canvas no longer. Then back in my small attic room, in a charming house close to the school, I would continue my searches further into the night. Then would follow talks, into the early hours of the morning, with Colin Sykes who shared this small flat with me. Those rooms bear within their walls much that is relevant and important to religion, art, and literature, from those delightful hours of talk. I owe much to Colin for his encouragement of my writing and much to him as a close friend interested in many of the same matters as myself, who made possible a communion of thought in a world mainly comprised of chalk, cricket bats and sweaty rugger shirts. This world I loved too; my mind re-acted generously to many aspects of school life, none more than the sight of small white-clad figures, still, against the dark green grass. I cannot pass on from Colin without mentioning an image which wholly symbolises this great friend of mine; it is a picture I have of a young, tall and distinguished-looking figure refereeing a football match nicely protected by a black umbrella.

My mind was flooded from many sources, none more important at the time than the pictorial images of the magic paintings which the children did in art class, and was greatly excited as these gorgeously created figures, patterns, signs and symbols flowed from the children on to paper. I have memory of a thousand miraculous inventions, born of child delight, and in a fashion that only they can conjure. Scenes ranging from 'The Earthquake' to 'A Music Lesson', and back to 'The Final Try' and 'How's That?'.

Two remain vividly in mind. The first is a large portrait, covering the acreage of a door, of a woman 'cellist who had recently given a memorable recital to the school. Adam Hart-Davis, at that time, might well have turned his back on his father's world of publishing, and gone forth as a painter. What an image! It was larger than life size, and oh so true to the subject matter.

The second scene occurred in the 'break' one morning, between two painting classes. One of my pupils, the only girl in the school, a gifted ten-year-old painter, had done a large and beautiful picture called 'Easter Breakfast'. It was hanging in a place of honour in the art room. It was entirely finished as far as I could see. But during the 'break' Veronica approached me shyly and said, "Excuse me, sir, but could I just finish my Easter Breakfast?" "But it's finished," I said, "You'll spoil it if you do anything more." "Please, sir . . . there's just *one* thing I want to do." I followed her into the art room while she delved in the cupboard for a tin of paint. She brought out a large tin of chrome yellow and a thin long brush. Dipping the brush into some water, she streaked in some yellow. "I forgot to butter the toast," she said. It was a delightful moment, reflecting the 'realism' desired by young children when painting and yet which, so often, does not obscure their instinctive poetic expression.

4

One more scene must be recorded, both for its stabilising effect upon my emotions and as a symbol of preparatory school life. The scene is a long wooden table, with ten boys decorating each side. Either end is punctuated by an adult, the matron and myself. The time is 8.10 a.m., school breakfast in the boys' dining room. I have arrived late, wearing dark glasses to avoid the distinct glare of a new day, the early part of which has absorbed me, in my attic flat, painting and writing. The glasses also help to adjust the colour range of the debris smudged across the boys' plates. Smeared egg yolk is nicely turned to the tanned delights of the Côte d'Azur. It is the only possible solution, visually, to such a scene. I might add that the glasses were only a secondary precaution, as usually my eyes were scarcely open during that breakfast session. Suddenly a voice from the far end of the table barks, "Finish up your fat." This order, issuing from the matron, in fact aimed at pupils on either side of me, sends me scurrying round *my* plate, finishing *my* fat. Breakfast was indeed a great ordeal for me. But as I say, these necessary disciplines did me as much good as the boys, kept my soul in order and my plate well cleaned.

By now I had become deeply involved with the painting of landscape. Having 'finished up my fat' for nearly two years, I felt the need of a more isolated life with a real and permanent home of my own, away from where I taught. Through the help of Margaret Brooke, who lived not far from where I taught, I was able to purchase a delightful, seventeenth-century cottage perched proudly at the top of Noakes Hill—and which, given a firm push, would have rolled down this hill, dangerously crossed a road at the bottom, and crashed into a field of wheat during summer. It was an idyllic place in which to work, geographically perfect in relation to the countryside, and was the 'rose-covered cottage' of my Athenian dreams. Here I became a serious painter of landscape. Here I bred long-haired black cats, and on one occasion shared their supper of Kit-E-Kat, when the larder was bare and

deep snow prevented excursion to the village. Here I worked towards my first exhibition of paintings, shown in Oxford in May
1954. Here I learnt the rare qualities of Margaret Brooke, which
I had discerned as a boy when first my family moved to Berkshire. She lived two fields away and helped me constantly, and in
particular when my legs went wrong. At Noakes Hill Cottage I
first realised I was essentially a painter of landscape, and that my
mind was most severely rocked by this aspect of nature.

At first it was a time of peace. My work, at any rate for the
first six months, was calm and objective. I worked almost entirely in gouache, and restricted my palette to black, white and
blue. This symbolises the realisation, which had dawned on me,
for the need of strict discipline. I applied this discipline to my
work and it progressed; but life was not yet ready to accept such
monastic strictness and thus I cannot claim the same order in its
day-to-day activities.

I worked in close collaboration with nature. My spirits soared
as I crouched in the hedgerows and rapidly sketched my notes.
Again I felt the link of hands, mind and body with something
much greater than myself. Away into the trees my mind floated
and my hand seemed linked both with the pencil and those
fiercely gesticulating branches. The calm period of objective work
moved into more passionate fields and the stubble of corn pierced
through the soles of my sandals, right up my tender aching legs,
into swelling thighs, up into my stomach and out into both
ecstatic hands, which for a moment seemed to hold the blue
eternal sky. As a fielder in cricket leaps up and seizes that whizzing
small dark ball, so did I, in those cornfields and hedgerows,
reach up and catch something of the eternal sun. Rare and
precious days they were, when first I met winter hedgerows face
to face, and upon their own terms. There is no compromise to
hedgerows, fierce summer corn, dark gesticulating winter elms,
nor to swollen waters which have broken the banks of their
flowing streams. For the first time I realised the full force and re-
silience of nature, and in its countless faces I saw the reflection of

God, a God of a million graces and favours, of limitless energy and power, at times stern and unbending, at others gentle as a snowflake and as exquisite as a weeping willow. In fences and trees, barns and sheds, moss and leaves, I found a light and joy which is inseparable from any true image of God. But slowly this image became tarnished and the glow faded. The pain in my legs was increasing, the muchi from the ulcers linking themselves to the fungi which had at first so much delighted me, and which decorated the bases of so many trees. Slowly the fusion of these 'sores' became so closely joined in my mind, and the pain bit in with a savagery which I had never associated with fungi, that the glowing aspects of nature darkened, and disappeared. There were left only beautifully disgusting patches of growth upon the trees, and increasingly ugly sores upon my feet. I felt now that a wood-pecker beat throbbed through these decorated clumps, striking at the tree roots, just as the stabs shot through my feet aiming at the marrow of my ankle bones.

Hospital was looming; my legs were interfering severely with my life. I decided to accept the operations advised and made arrangements to enter hospital. The future seemed very bleak and was echoed in the raindrops which stuttered drunkenly down the sixteen sad windows of the ward. It was again like the first day at boarding school; I was an 'outsider' and everything was strange. I remember clambering into a cold virginlike bed and the screens being moved away to reveal a view of the ward which I should never know again. It was that first look which a room reveals to a newcomer and which slips away without notice, and is perhaps, just for a second, caught again in a tired or very special moment. It is a world seen clearly and entirely objectively, with no sub-jective strain. For three months it was to be my world.

It was a relief to be off my aching, ulcered legs. It was a com-fort to have soothing dressings put on by someone else, as neatly applied as bandages on the hocks of horses' legs. It was good to know that further treatment might aid them. I opened my diary and began jotting down the memories of the past few weeks.

It was a weekend when I entered the hospital. A calm had descended upon it; the ward was full of badly damaged people but even their damage, and the necessary repair, seemed to have come to a standstill. Legs hung on pulleys, raised beds (mine was one of them), plastered arms, bandaged heads, all seemed suspended in time and space. There was a certain smugness in the ward; it was as if nothing would ever change. This gave me a feeling of security. I rested as much on the negativity of those first few hours as upon my bed and pillows. Slowly, over the weekend, as my dressings were done, I melted into the ward and became a part of it.

It is the details within a ward which build the whole. Lying in bed, there is a world of time to think and speculate, to dream and hope. Hope is the operative word; there is a distinct feeling of very real hope within a surgical ward. From my bed I was able to study the details miscroscopically, from the flowers by the bed-side to the slippers on the floor, and back to the distorted shapes of plastered limbs and figures.

I noticed the hairs on my legs in a way I had never done before; I was struck by their darkness and their insistence, their effort. I noticed my face in quite a different way, in the mirror, while I shaved. Every detail registered, The bandages on my feet were different too, possessing the calm practicality of the ward. My hands became more important for I was reliant upon them, while in bed, a great deal. I learnt which movements and leanings would help my comfort in the bed. This was to be very important after the operations, when movement was severely limited for ten days. During that weekend I learnt again the frustration of being confined to bed. I felt like a toy electric train, turned upside down, with the wheels left spinning.

As evening approached, and the windows darkened, the ward itself became confined. The backcloth was changed and the centre of the stage was again the ward. My slippers seemed so still and patient lying beside the bed. The sheets became white against the darkening light outside; movements in the beds were more accentuated.

There was an exquisite bunch of roses blooming on the table in front of me. A man was screened to my right. We all knew he was dying. As night approached his groans became deeper and fuller. The movement of nurses became more regular and busy behind the screens, there were strange shadows from behind them, shapes appeared and disappeared upon the wall.

The movement of the nurses and the shadows playing high on the wall made me think of a dramatic dance. A theme occurred to me for a ballet; it grew from the contrast between rose and patient. Instead of a dying man, there would be a pregnant mother. As her condition deteriorated, so the flowers in the ward would bloom more beautifully. The mother's dance would be effected by shadow play behind the screens. There would be a still, dramatic movement, in the operating theatre, when flower and patient would both be suspended. Soon afterwards the woman would die giving birth to a child, the flower supreme at this moment. Then quite suddenly the cry of a new-born child would be heard and the flower would wither and die. Human life would again be supreme.

So ran my thoughts during that terrible night. The fierce ballet persisted till the early hours of the morning, when with one terrible animal grunt the patient was silent. The chorus of nurses persisted, the ward was filled with horror; death had come to it and only a few feet from the two of us on either side of the screens.

The flowers continued their graceful blooming when brought back next morning. The screens were brusquely parted and the deceased patient emerged, thinly disguised by a Union Jack. All his pain and recent twisted agony was expressed in the folds of that covering, the red speaking for his frozen blood, the white stripe cool and ironic, and the blue matching perfectly the Sister's dark uniform. Where had that flag spent its last few days? What other functions had it riotously witnessed, fluttering at full mast, and what date had it exchanged its glorious duties for this sacred one? And whose choice had that been? The little brown major, with the grey moustache and a permanent stoop? Or had it always been preserved for such an occasion as this, when it could ironically re-echo glory, life and death in a battlefield of ridges, in transparently pale form?

The pomp accorded to the occasion contrasted vividly with the words of the nurse on my left. "Have you had your bowels open today?" she asked. "Like hell I have nurse, a proper deluge it was," came the reply.

The ward was soon a healing ground for the rest of us and operations began again on Monday. I was not amongst this batch; my op. was for Wednesday. Two days to prepare for it.

I was awakened very early on the Wednesday morning with a cup of tea and two thin pieces of toast. Five a.m. Two hours later a hive of activity buzzed round the bed; shaving, preparation, bandaging. It all seemed to happen in a rush. It reminded me of an impromptu rugger scrum. I was trussed like a chicken and left lying on my back to consider the situation, the ball rather than a player.

The operation, to improve the circulation in my legs, was a stomach one; which seemed strange, considering that it was my legs which needed attention, but apparently it was necessary. The details had been explained to me. I tried not to let my imagination roam too far.

Cheerful words, coarse jokes, general ribaldry broke out when my bed was screened. It was as if paper darts, inscribed with greeting card messages, mixed up with dirty postcards, had suddenly cascaded into the air. They helped break the tension and suspense. I began to feel heroic and important. I lay back and relaxed because I felt that that was expected of me; sort of "Carry on, Sergeant-major, don't worry about me, get the men out at all costs. . . ." But I was very frightened. Sweat covered the palms of my hands. Occasionally I threw back a flippant joke and hoped it sounded really nonchalant. I was more frightened of seeming frightened. It would be terrible to be thought a coward in this ward. I longed to be as brave and dashing and bold as they all were. The green curtained screens seemed very green, the ward itself very far away.

A nurse came to give me an injection. I asked her what it was. 'It's Omnaponscopolamine,' she replied brightly. It was good to know that such a magic and poetic-sounding fluid was to aid me. I picked up my diary and wrote down the name as soon as the nurse had left me. I continued writing in the diary, whilst a faint sensation of remoteness crawled round my body. I felt like a knight on a chessboard, who has been picked up for some forward attacking movement and then been returned, after hesitation, to the same square. I began to feel very grown-up. In a way it was like the first scent of a strong tobacco which I had been given by a middle-aged man in the ward a few nights before. I had suddenly, for a moment, become part of that mature and ruggedly handsome middle-aged man. I even felt my hair to be almost white.

Decisions were taken from me gradually and gently. I continued the diary notes, feeling a daredevil boldness in this action, a Scott of the Antarctic strength of purpose. I remember my pipe on the locker beside me, it seemed absurdly rich and mature. My finger nails were very pink and the crescent moon shapes, at their base, much whiter than usual. The ones on my two thumbs were the size of cumulus clouds. In the mirror, which I fetched into the bed, I saw a pale, slightly drawn face with very dark eyes and sparkling hair. It looked dangerously attractive. The picture in the mirror was like a Dali painting, slightly out of focus.

I became more and more hazy; my mouth dried up; I remember the screens being parted and two nurses helping me on to a trolley stretcher with the aid of a male assistant. It was a smooth and satisfying journey out of the ward, covered by warm furry blankets right up over my face. Only my nose and eyes were peeping through. I felt like a submarine with its conning tower just peeping through the surface of the water. We turned corners, up a ramp, and came to a standstill. Then I remember a man bending over me, with a nurse nearby, and a voice which seemed very far away. He held a needle in his hand; I remember the prick and three seconds later a swirling sensation swamped my whole being. I whirled into darkness. . . .

When next I opened my eyes the ward was dark. I did not know where I was. Everything was out of focus and when I moved slightly in the bed a scorching pain shot through my stomach. The pain, when I coughed, was excruciating. I remember the screens round my bed, a nurse murmuring something, and then more sleep. When I awoke, I found the ward bright and there was much activity going on around my screened bed. I was given a drink of very sweet orange juice and then I slept, on and off, for most of the day. In the evening the pain seared through me again and I was given a shot of morphia. Soon I floated out of pain, via crimson fields of crying poppies, into a world free of colour, care or dimension—nothingness.

The sensation of the increased flow of blood in my left leg was alarming in a way. The satisfaction gave way to a feeling of panic, fright that the pulsing flow might be too much for the arteries and veins, and would burst through the skin. I imagined a fire-hose spurt of scarlet blood gushing into the bottom of my bed which nothing would stop. I was glad that I could move my legs so little. Any false move might start this cascade.

Obviously no such dramatic thoughts occurred to the surgeon when he visited me the next day. As he turned to the Sister and said, "Well, that's fine, we'll do the other one in a month's time," I was reminded of a plumber wiping his hands in satisfaction after mending one of the pipes, before he turns his attention to the trivially blocked wash-basin.

At first, as I lay flat on my back, the bed tray cut across my eyes like a knife clenched between some giant's teeth. It grinned widely at me and covered, in span, three and a half beds. It symbolised

4*

the limited world which I inhabited. From this confinement my imagination stretched far and wide, scaled by the looming shapes close to my eyes. Through these unusual and disturbing proportions, which forced themselves right down my throat, I judged the world. Everything, in relation to the vast bridge across my stomach, the huge cups and apples which rested upon it, was diminutive and without significance, a mere backcloth to the giant world in which I lay. Consequently it was only possible to judge the remainder of the ward as an extension of the backcloth against which I lived. It was a simple matter to float out, supreme and confident, into a universe so much smaller than myself and lacking its third and most important dimension. They were hazy but happy journeys which I made from my bed, my eyes often Cyclops-integrated into one, as I squinted into the foreground objects and tried to widen beyond them.

Lying in bed during those ten days affected my mind in an extraordinary fashion. I was mainly a passive spectator to a world of surrealist conversations and sights, whilst I lay perspiring, and the zip-fastener slits across my stomach gradually fastened themselves together. I worked in top gear, after the first three days, writing furiously to stave off the pain, and most of it was subdued by this concentrated effort. I became a silent tape-recorder, recording the world of the ward. My mind was acutely alert, spinning with ideas, which generated to profusion with the strict confinement. This high fling of the pendulum stemmed from three vital sources; emotions fully released by the success of the operation which I had feared so much, unbounding hope and plans for the future, and the cross parry of razor-sharp ward wit across my bed. This particular form of wit, a heightened form of the barrack-room type, is partly born from the exhibitionist powers of man, partly as an answer to an uncertain situation; it is used, in its thrust, as armour. It splintered across my bed, showering me in its glowing segments, flaming my mind and igniting my whole nervous and mental system. I was suddenly immersed in pure mental activity, with no outlet for my physical energies.

Most of the men in the ward, and I was one of them, spoke of their pains, their stitches, their cases, as if the world orbited around them. As if the world would burst if their stitches did, or stop if their 'tickers' failed. We told the doctors and nurses which pains were worse or better, and pin-pointed their moves—'no, just there, nurse'—and they gave us assurance and pills, and puffed up our pillows. And for a short time our pains were better. We would tell one nurse (probably more) our whole case history, then sleep for an hour, only to find a new nurse on duty, who actually did not know we had that particular pain in the small of our back or far right toe.

The actual notes which I made in my diary at that time are lost. but I will quote another 'accelerated thought' process, recorded during a recent spell in hospital for further leg operations, when again the total forces within me were funnelled into my mind, through a long period of immobilisation upon my back. During the latter part of this recent hospital period, I slept very little, and (until stopped by the night staff) was in the habit of reading and writing by the light from the street below, which was close to Waterloo Station. The particular sequence quoted was made towards the end of this three month 'retreat', and sums up some of the ideas which were fermenting within me.

During this particular night I had been re-reading John Custance's book *Wisdom, Madness and Folly*; we had been in communication recently through letters; in fact the last letter was the book mark to the chapter I was reading, 'A Universe of Bliss'. I felt not only in close communion with John Custance, through memories of a happy luncheon sparkling with laughter and aided by two fine bottles of claret, which we had recently shared in Dorset, but also I felt in synchronistic contact through the endless flow of my ideas and my state of bliss, which married perfectly with John's descriptions of this vitally charged and extraordinary sensation.

My mind wandered round the words INK POT, which John had selected as an important incident during a heightened state, when these two words had suggested to him, not the dipping in of his pen, but the biological function of the lavatory. Rapid thought associations took place, within my accelerated mind, around this adjective and noun; ink pot, children's potty, not so 'potty', ink pot function (dipping into), dipping, Piero della Francesca's 'Baptism of Christ', cleansing, cleaning the body, excreta, lavatory. It seemed to me quite obvious why these two words were linked with this biological function; I felt this to be a more accurate interpretation than Freud might have made, in his earlier years, possibly linking 'the pen dipping' with sexual intercourse. With lavatory, and sexual intercourse, in my mind, it was no great distance to another form of 'giving up', in both the death-wish and death itself. And, as if by synchronicity, the faint beam of the torch illumined a newspaper heading near my elbow:

OBITUARY.
Louis Macneice.
Verse with brisk, lively ring.

My mind galloped on. It seemed a cryptic comment upon a poet of his distinction. A cryptic comment which suggested immediately to me the gestures of Charlie Chaplin and Tony Hancock, with their brevity and perception, exposing, in a flash, man's weakness, dignity and pomp. Perception, Signs, symbols; Steinberg's penetrating observations upon modern man and society in his beautiful drawings and cartoons; James Thurber, Walter Mitty, man's need of myth, *Cat and Mouse* (a novel I was reading), Lewis Carroll, surrealism, the unconscious, Freud, Jung, mysticism, religion, Christianity, the Trinity, Christ, perception, necessity in perception for the marriage of three senses, eyes (looking), ears (listening), action (translation), need for action being positive, action stations, alarm, emergency ward, compassion, pity and positive action, concern, like Dickens for the unprivileged ones, Rembrandt's compassionate understanding in his portraits, the reading of faces, palms of hands, perception through signs and symbols, strewn everywhere for the looking, the reading of signs, road signs, communication, telepathy, extra sensory perception, mind over matter, core, heart, beat, generate, electricity, wireless, radio without wires, no connection, 'look no hands!', free wheeling, free will, God, the unknown source of power and life, or magic. What is magic? Surely the profoundest interpretation by man, through that 'unknown' power which enables him to add the sum total of his experiences, TO life.

I then formulated a 'Test team' of twelve players whom I thought had brought magic to the world. The torch was fading rapidly, so that I had not time to select as carefully as I should have liked. I record what was scribbled in my diary during those last flickers of the torch:

1st XI or Test Team.

1. Rembrandt.
2. Jung.
3. Leonardo da Vinci.
4. Galileo.
5. Our Lord.
6. Piero della Francesca.
7. Goya.
8. Shakespeare.
9. Jean Jacques Rousseau.
10. Goethe.
11. Plato.
12th man. Robert Frost.

I then scribbled, 'Whom have I left out? Some very great players I'm sure, and some lesser ones who deserve notice, like Mr. Parrish.' (Mr. Parrish was a working man who had just left the ward, and to me had reflected in his courage, simplicity and lack of complaint in his years of suffering, Our Lord himself.) I continued in the diary: 'Re-arrange batting order tomorrow and try and get the priorities right.' This example of thought associa-

tion, and its results, shows not only the pattern of a high pendulum swing, but also the proximity of thought towards Good;
always during these swings, I am fervently pulled towards ideals
and qualities far beyond my capacity, and my thoughts linked to
Christ, Saints and the creative giants of the past and present.

The days at Roehampton, while recovering from the operation,
piled on to each other as blackberries do during a picking session,
the basket suddenly fuller than expected. I learned, during the
ten days before the stitches were removed, to live a different sort
of life, where my hands played an important part and my sense of
balance and judgement of distances were of prime importance. I
became a part of a world whose very real democracy was only
unbalanced by another form of 'superiority'; a man's rank, with
some justice I think, was reckoned by the number and seriousness
of operations and diseases which he had had.

A surgical ward is the world on a small scale, a surrealist world
which exposes man in a clear way. Man's courage is seen, his
determination, his inventiveness, his fears, phobias, fantasies,
dreams, his strength and his weakness.

My reactions to people and objects contrasted strongly before
the operation and after it. When I entered the ward, I was brimful
of fears and doubts, the emotions which strangle our lives so constantly. They were negative, in the sense that my emotional state
did not really allow for objective thought. As an example of this,
I can quote my reaction to objects (as in Greece), which was
mainly one-sided and prejudiced by my own emotional state. As
before, I imbued objects with my particular momentary problems. A group of simple objects on a bedtable, a glass, an apple, a
newspaper, a pipe, when pushed away from a bed into the middle
of the ward, became a symbol of man's potential isolation. Another locker, loaded with fruit, cigarettes and chocolates reminded
me of our self-indulgence. They reminded and embarrassed me.
It was not until after the operation, when I led an almost ascetic
life for ten days, that I perceived the duality and paradox of our

natures, through simple objects. Later, through this duality, I was reminded of many other paradoxes which fence across our lives; our love of life, the death-wish; our love so closely 'cained' to hate, courage and fear; our dreams and despairs; our light and our darkness; Doctor Jekyll and Mr. Hyde. Innocent as it may sound, the great truth of our paradoxical nature never dawned on me until after the operation, although the germs had been sown (and entirely misunderstood) in that Athens ward. After the operation I realised, in a flash, the importance of our duality, or in the words of Captain Franklin, late of the Pioneer Corps, 'You've got to take the rough with the smooth', to which a sentimental cockney added, 'Every cloud has a silver lining.'

According to my mood, during the days before the operation, I saw flowers as the symbol of eternal glory, or as the symbol of our frailty. The pendulum, as usual, swung between extremes. I did not sense the possible marriage of the two states; I was in no condition to do so. Certainly the immensely difficult balance of the two states had never dawned on me; until I watched the ward scales being used, to which I referred in Chapter Two.

Inspiration is an unpopular word these days. I think in its denial is a reflection of modern man's inability to recognise anything more important than himself. I now understand some part of it, as being the magic link which marries cause and effect, subconscious and conscious thought, so that there are not two separate entities but one blinding whole. I experienced, lying frustrated on my back, the sort of blinding flash of certainty which struck St. Paul on the road to Damascus, when black and white, good and evil, were as sharply separated and linked as the two opposing dishes had been on the ward scales.

It was as if a voice was speaking to me through these objects. At Roehampton, it was the opposite of the Greek drawing experience, when a stream of drawings and thoughts had reflected, through objects, my particular emotional problems. But both experiences shared a clarity of perception and unexpected attendance of powers which I really did not know I possessed, igniting within me, from an 'unknown source' which I take to be God's; the positive nature of these experiences is similar to the recognition of Grace, as known to the Roman Catholic Church. That there is a link, I feel certain; the important matter to realise, and which took me some years to discover, is that Grace, or the high pendulum swing, is a privileged bestowal whose powers must be used for positive and practical purpose. Under the high swing, it is easy to behave like a man who has just won the football pools; for indeed so great is one's pleasure, one's ecstasy, one's love for everybody and everything, that it is a simple matter to lose perspective in the everyday world, in an effort to bestow upon it items and ideas which just do not interest it. It is a bursting and bestowing sensation of gargantuan proportions.

It was as if I stood apart from my words and thoughts; my answers to questions, often upon subjects little known to me, possessed the kind of certainty and understanding which I associated with Christ in the Temple as a boy. I possessed for a short while the full force of order, reason and logic, which manifested itself in lightning thought association and the interpretation of objects.

I remember another everyday ward activity which spoke to me with special meaning. A nurse was cutting some soft pink lint with a large pair of scissors close to my bed. I was a little drugged against my pain, and as I dreamily watched these scissors snip, snapping into the lint, they became a fiercely glinting pair of crocodile jaws. The two jaws represented our dual natures, our animus and anima, our contradictions and contensions: the frictions of life. As the nurse laid the scissors upon the table, her task finished, the two jaws were united into one pointed shape, a finely unified and positive blade. There had been marriage. It was then that the small miracle occurred. From this marriage and the fierce contensions of the previous few minutes had appeared two neat piles of soft pink lint. A pair of twins had been born; indeed it was a miraculous world, I thought, noticing the blood bottle above the man opposite me, as I dozed off to sleep.

The blood bottle, hung on a simple wooden cross, also spoke to me in two ways. At first, on entering the ward, I had been frightened of this blood-transfusion bottle, and the cross which carried it was a clear warning of Our Lord's suffering. The crimson blood emphasised this image of sacrifice and suffering. But as a child discovers that a flame will hurt his hand by experience, so one learns in a hospital ward to accept objects and situations which are, on their face value, terrible or ugly, because they may help one. Man, with his innate sense of fear, is usually frightened of anything which he does not understand. But the blood bottle became my friend, and I saw the symbol of agony and torment transformed into a resplendent crimson which reminded me of those great and gorgeous apples which Courbet painted and now hang in the National Gallery. The fullness of the bottle, too, reminded of Courbet's sense of ripeness, and as it emptied I felt the disappointment, known in childhood days, of a favourite conker suddenly lost from a trouser pocket. The wooden cross itself changed its message; now it became a combination or the two extremes in movement, the marrying of the vertical and the horizontal. In place of crossed forms and anguish was peace and perfection.

This last image, the cross and its dual nature, led to a flash of understanding that this symbol was the only one which Christ could have chosen for us; it seemed to me, in that ward, that it was just another form of synchronicity which led the Romans to choose this particular method of execution. The Romans and Christ seemed to me to have selected the most perfect symbol for mankind, which spoke of anxiety, dark suffering and the contradiction of our natures in the same voice that it sang of visual perfection through the marriage of two opposing movements. It struck me that man too often reads only one aspect into an image; it is well known to psychologists that a state of anxiety produces, often, the crossing and cancellation of forms. I remembered this well from the time when I had taught maladjusted children painting; often, in an unhappy child, a row of houses would be contradicted by some trees running right through them. But, I thought in that Roehampton ward, surely it is another expression of man's fear that, usually, he chooses the suffering image in the cross. Surely the story of the Crucifixion, in fact and in symbolism, is best understood as one of duality, extreme suffering and perfection of balance.

I had not before shared an operation with a ward full of people. We 'out-opped' each other continuously, and I learnt not only the skills of this game from men far more damaged than I was, but much about our self-indulgence, and I heard the hollow echoes of the death-wish in the morbid conversations around me.

The pendulum reacted swiftly to this atmosphere. Relief that the operation was over, and the vitality of the continuous repartee around me, had swept my mind into sharply facetious and associative humour. Associative ideas pour one upon another, words parry and marry with each other, sentences flow one into another, so that I am filled to bursting with the kind of sharp dialogue so well known on the music halls, where one word is picked and immediately links itself to another not perceived a second before. It is the razor-sharp wit of the Cockney Jew, self-protective and at times prenetrating, often merely facetious and possibly crude. I do not kid myself that my blasé Etonian accent changes the content of this repartee; it merely adds a certain elegance, and to undiscerning ears, a sophistication quite separated from the East End joker. But I know exactly where the link lies and where the armour of this wit was forged.

Ironically, despite the severe operations, the ward at Roehampton brought a fitness to my system which I had not known since childhood. Consequently I loosed myself into work, seizing this 'inspirational moment' for what it was worth. I am sad that I have destroyed the two notebooks in which I must have scrawled some twenty or thirty thousand words during those ten days in bed, recording the world of that ward. I am sure there were perceptive pieces of writing amongst the chaff, for I was, as in

Greece, in a highly receptive state. But I have memories worth recording, most of which are connected with the heightened visual sense and the symbolic clarity of objects.

As I have mentioned, the scissors spoke to me forcibly. I felt too the significance of the 'ghost pain' in a man's amputated leg, when he could feel the missing toes itching and the lower limb flexing. It seemed to me that this extension of the nerves proved something more than mere fact of nerve reaction. It seemed a direct link with the world of ghosts and vanished spirits, proof of the extension of ourselves in time and space after death.

My mind raced back to the pruning of roses and their strengthened blooms later in the year, to animals divided and continuing life, such as worms. I seemed to understand something beyond natural science and the laws exposed by Darwin; I sensed, in a strange but definite way, that his theories were only an infinitesimal part of the story. I seemed to stand close to the eternal part of man which death cannot destroy. I knew, for certain, that there was an afterlife, in some form or other.

The accelerated succession of thoughts upon this subject illustrates well, I think, the pendulum mind when it is swinging freely. From nerve pains, ghosts and vanished spirits, my mind seized first upon the accepted idea that the past nerve sensations are permanently stored or photographed in some part of the brain. This would confirm the ghost pain in a leg no longer linked to the body. But my mind was not content with this scientific or medical explanation and it reached out for further answers. I saw first the alive brain as a vast record office, file upon file of not altogether well arranged card indexes and memos. This rather too efficient civil service department, so zealous in its enthusiasm for records at any cost, soon turned to a laboratory filled with a group of almost hysterical, white-coated, long-haired young scientists poring over each fresh 'nerve reaction plate' with such intensity and possessiveness that the designer of the room had allowed no windows or doors in case of possible leakage. How the scientists entered this room never worried me.

And obviously they never desired to leave it. The room was overflowing with activity and the plates leapt and jostled for priority of viewing, then quite suddenly collapsed in exhaustion and lay as if dead. Only the occasional flicker of an eyelid confirmed life in these flattened forms. And that in itself might have been merely latent nerve reaction.

I was forced to rest in a mental hospital four years later and again I had the chance to re-value life. Between all these experiences, and through the wisdom of several close friends, I have learnt something of the complexities of life and a deal of useful self-knowledge. Any knowledge I have of psychology has been born mainly of these experiences. As a superb example of many facets of psychological disturbance, I have scarcely needed to read text books, though I am often fascinated, when reading such books, to find proof of what I have experienced first hand. Jung in particular has aided me in a much deeper self-knowledge, as he must anyone who believes in the close link of the mystical with medicine and science.

If I had acted upon the philosophy which reached out to me from such hours of looking, listening and learning at Roehampton, I should have become a wise and balanced person. I watched flowers unfold and close, bloom and die, registering their particular rhythms and lack of haste. I too, through my physical limitations, responded to the natural functions and rhythms of nature and accordingly healed surely and quickly. As I have mentioned before, pain and illness force one back to animal instincts of self-preservation; this I had first sensed whilst lying near to death in Greece. Again after the leg operations, I learnt my limitations and flowed with the stream rather than against it. In the same way as you can learn to relax by watching a cat sprawled in front of the fire, or how to sit correctly by watching a child, so I learnt from flowers, and from other damaged people, which movements were the natural and unstrained ones. I re-discovered my body in a sublime way, not narcissicistly, but as an instrument, which if used correctly could do infinite things. It was the joy an agile child finds on the playing fields when his body responds to pure movement. The joy a lamb must feel in skipping. Nothing more complicated than that. And as I learnt to walk correctly again, without a limp, I re-lived days which I had known instinctively as a boy and youthful athlete. This in itself gave me an immense sense of power, not a complex power, but a force of sheer exhilaration in being alive, with a mind which was linked perfectly to it. I lived in harmony with myself during that hospital period.

One afternoon, lying in a hazy stupor of pains and pills, I noticed a handsome blue book on the locker adjacent to mine. As I dozed off to sleep, it linked itself to the memory of the scales and scissors; dreamily it worked itself into my mind and when I awoke I found myself immersed in this object, somehow connected with the Trinity, through duality. The symbol of duality was contained in the cover, the strong, firm front and back of the book representing two separate poles. Their link was only possible through the content of the white pages which pregnantly joined them together; the raison d'être of that book lay in those pages, which gave birth to ideas and thoughts. It was a perfect trinity of purpose and as satisfying to me, at that time, as Raphael's classic and perfect Madonna. And so my mind wandered from object to object, the pain submerged entirely by a miraculous world of signs and symbols which were strewn all over the ward. Scarcely an object did not possess some fascination or quality which stirred my mind to deeper matters.

It was thus that I discovered the link of man's symbols with God's. Something, as I have said before, which started hysterically in Greece, without full comprehension, and which was to change the course of my work and thinking. But this did not occur, directly, for a few years.

My father had sent me a large tin of my favourite tobacco. It was beautifully round. It opened with that delightful puff of exhaustion which is the habit of sealed tins. Inside was a ruff of paper exquisitely folded in neat creases. It was just like the ruff of a seventeenth-century Dutch lady such as Rembrandt painted. I scarcely dared disturb it. I thought of the ingenious machine which would have stamped out this pattern and shape and marvelled that it should bother. In the centre, the sienna and black wisps peeped through. There was a round white notice on top which lifted off to reveal the ruff and tobacco, and on it was printed "GUARANTEE. This tobacco is guaranteed to be made from the purest leaf, naturally matured and free from artificial flavouring and adulterants of any kind. It is identical wherever purchased, at home or abroad. If you have any cause for complaint kindly return this tin to your retailer." I certainly had no cause for complaint, I longed to write and tell what delight the whole tin, and its opening, had given me. I saw the 'purest leaf', tissue thin, growing in some far-off tobacco field, in a scorching land. I wondered what an adulterant was; I was sure this tin suffered from no such complaint.

I put the tobacco into my black pouch and then dug conspiratorially into it while filling the pipe. I lit my pipe and watched the match die down and wither into the ashtray beside me, black and a dash of whitey yellow wood. A dramatic sight, alone on the ashtray.

I could not move much in bed without pain, so that it was necessary to collect everything around within easy distance. It became like a game of snooker, to push and persuade objects away or towards me. Just a pencil and with a few taps of it I could dispense with a bottle of ink, and with a lasso of my handkerchief I could summon an apple or orange just out of reach. I received great pleasure from 'ordering' the objects around me by the most ingenious movements which I could devise, and thus keeping myself supplied with the necessary things for my hour-to-hour needs.

If you look at a surgical ward carefully and without bias, you will find an extraordinary range of beautiful objects. There is good reason for this; most of the objects are entirely utilitarian, designed for a very specific purpose, and consequently they have a beauty and simplicity; they are not fake in any way. Medicine bottles, simple white plates, crutches, pulleys, bed rails, curtain knobs, bed trays, ward tea-pots, are just a few of the objects which delighted me. I found splendour in the curved pair of earphones lying on the bedtable in front of me with an apple just touching the headpiece. A plug looked fine and resplendent with its wire straggling away over the edge of the table. Pillows were magnificent, clean sheets an eternity of peace. The blue and white of the nurses' uniform possessed the same simple distinction as the Guards' blue and scarlet and the black and white of evening dress. It occurred to me then that in England our uniforms are the best in the world because they are so simple and employ just two main colours. I was fascinated by the ever-moving veils of the nurses which added elegance and a particular significance to all their movements. The poetry of the veil has been a constant source of spiritual and sensual delight during difficult times in hospital. It has seemed to have the power of healing within it, a symbol of cleansing, perfection and peace. There are few faces which are not almost beatified by it.

A pendulum mind works too fast. It responds not only in ecstasy, which is in itself a power and flight of such swiftness and upsurge that it cannot even be considered in relation to the accepted meaning of movement; it is part of the momentum force of life itself, more powerful than a sudden swirl of wind, more flighty than a thousand skylarks soaring in the sky; it has not the spectral force of a gale and yet knows its intensity and is no more able to stem its flow than the sun can frost its rays.

Ward conversation, the indulgent sort, fired my imagination and often I recorded memories of it, late in the evening, with its reflections and echoes of man's state still ringing in my mind. I quote one of these jottings, exactly as it was made at the time, to show the activity of my mind and as a faithful record of a typical ward conversation. I have of course changed the patient's name. I must admit that I was capable at that time, or now for that matter, of holding such a monologue myself. Indeed I often have. The words flowed on to the paper as I scribbled lying on my back. It was as if I snatched them from the air above my bed, where they hovered, permanently linked in my thoughts with all the objects around me.

"My name's Butler, Captain Ernest Butler. Been in here six weeks—you going to be long? Now take my case," and before I had had time to accept or reject 'his case', Captain Butler was in full swing again; "now take my case, four years ago they said it was hopeless, absolutely hopeless, not a chance in a thousand. Not a chance in a thousand. Then I was sent to see Mr. Carver, really through my uncle's wife's daughter, she was a nurse . . . well it was her who first mentioned Mr. Carver; and Mr. Carver says, 'Captain Butler, I'm interested in your case, very interested. I should like to do an . . .'"; at this point Captain Butler flashed a medical word of some six syllables, two of which rang with accentuated diphthongs, "I'd like to do it on Monday, that was four weeks ago yesterday, I beg your pardon, tomorrow; you get so confused with days in hospital after all this time." This last remark faded into the ward, attempting self-pity, but in fact swollen with pride for his four weeks' seniority and suffering. "So there I was for the 'chopper', not a bit nervous, but first of all, two days before the op; they did a lot of X-rays." At this moment his face lit with an enthusiasm rarely expressed by X-ray plates. "They've got a smashing set up there; they first of all pump in a lot of blue stuff, well you might say it was purple, I've always been a little colour blind, they first of all pump in a lot of this blue stuff into your arteries—only the ones they're going to X-ray of course—then they blow them up." At this last remark he seemed to grow larger and more important. "They did fourteen, that was in the afternoon, and six more next morning, which doesn't include the ones they'd done the first day I arrived."

At this point Captain Butler paused to allow his point, and the blue-cum-purple injections, to be fully injected. "You could tell they knew their job," again Captain Butler managed to effect the feeling that they had learnt this special knowledge for his benefit alone, "Oh they knew their job all right. It's a smashing set-up over there; of course it's a long journey but they take you by ambulance." Captain Butler was filled with delighted remembrance of that ambulance ride when he had been helped down the three steps by a fair, pretty nurse on arrival. "Now my boy's good at photography and all that sort of thing; you may think I'm boasting if I tell you he won the Tech. College prize for his colour photos—his Spanish holiday and all that—but it's a fact. Well when I told him about the set-up over there, in the X-ray department, you should have seen his face . . ."

Captain Butler's eyes misted over and he was back in that world of egocentrical, X-ray, seclusion, where his whole history of suffering was exposed, and permanently fixed by chemicals, on twenty semi-matt dark sheets of negative, and which, now that his Captain's rank was one of name and not authority, was his sole link with the world of importance; for a short time everything had revolved round him in a way that it had only done during the war. Consequently he treasured his disease most preciously and nursed it indulgently. His eyes unmisted a little and he continued, "Mind you, they can't do this op. on everyone, it just doesn't work." The last four words were uttered as if he had watched all the cases on which it had not worked. I saw body after body expiring, with blue-cum-purple-blood spurting, which no doctor could stem.

"But I was lucky; it was a risk mind you, but I took it," he added hastily, "now look at my legs; of course they'll never be the same . . . still . . ." and his voice faded.

In bed, as at the washing-up sink, you are stymied by the Captain Butlers of this world. But in these self-centred revelations, so indulgently told, there is a certain poetry, a poetry of revelation about the loneliness of the human animal and its desperate need for love and attention.

"So I says to Mr. Carver, if you really want to show my legs to the students, I mean if my small troubles can help the world in any way . . ."

After ten days, when the stitches had been removed, I was allowed up properly. As I rose from the bed and took my first step, I was reminded of that walk in the Greek ward almost ten years before, and the urine bottle goal I had scored. While tottering to the lavatory, it was strange to see the tops of tables, bird's-eye-view, which for ten days I had experienced as horizontal strips. The distance between my bed and the lavatory was another continent; I was an explorer discovering new lands. The imagined place was different from the discovered one. It was real, had three dimensions, and its own very special smell. My conquest of it produced its fourth dimension. Involvement with some place, thing or person gives me a fourth dimension. The pulling of the chain gave me much satisfaction (it was the raising of the 'flag'), and gave the bowl an entirely new and most needed look. It was a proud victor who staggered back to his bed, with the knowledge that a new and important land had been charted, in whose regions signs of habitation, even of intellectual learning, had been discerned. A piece of paper had floated to the floor, just as I was leaving, blown off some windowsill; on it was printed, "Now please wash your hands.' This was some message which would effect magic if complied with. The authority of it lay in those simple but firm five words. I was given orders in bed; messages could be received in that small, smelly room just out of the ward.

Soon I was moving about with ease and walking in the garden. I had noticed some cricket stumps arranged against the garden wall to encourage patients to 'limber up'. I envied their positive verticals and sureness. They were often the scene of rhythmic action and windmill arms. They contrasted entirely with my cramped and painful sensations; for a moment as the occupational therapist massaged my legs, with sure and firm movements, I became linked in spirit with those three fine stumps which represented all that was pure and fine and perfect. My eagerness to be healed and whole again, unified in the way they were, increased. I longed for them. I had temporarily lost the firmness sensed so clearly in the garden through the French windows, and was determined to regain it. A certain conflict grew within me, when I knew I must 'humiliate' those stumps, conquer them, and thus re-assert my full manhood. I longed to bowl a ball at terrific speed at them and send them flying.

My chance came about a fortnight later. Therapy had begun to put my muscles in trim again; I was ready for the first bowl. I picked up the hard, red ball and trotted down to the crease, and with as much force as I could summon, whizzed the ball towards the stumps. That first ball struck the centre stump and sent it staggering against the wall. My pleasure was enormous. All the pent-up frustration of the past few weeks was released in that piece of bowling, my accuracy (never to be repeated, as much as I bowled) was the result, I think, of continuous accurate study of weights, shapes, and forms while in bed. I shall always remember that piece of bowling, it seemed to come from the bottom of my bed, up through the sheets into my legs, right through my stomach into my right arm, out of the ward through the French windows and down the centre line. The stump was linked in some strange way with me and its blow as inevitable as the falling of a stone. I was fit again.

The first fortnight of leave was a happy period; it was good to be so fit again. Each day saw improvement in the legs. During the last fortnight of my leave the pendulum swung low; it was a strange feeling like nothing I had known before, quite different from my Greek experiences.

I became lethargic and could not eat, did not want to do anything, and had bad stomach pains. I put this down to the thought of returning to hospital, a subconscious reaction to returning to ward life again.

I returned to the hospital feeling suddenly very ill indeed. Perhaps I had overdone things, perhaps I should never have bowled that ball in the garden or exercised myself so much. The doctors were puzzled. Next day, after an appalling night, I was diagnosed as having jaundice.

I was moved to a side ward and isolated. I cared about nothing and felt very ill indeed. A thousand roses in full bloom or a Palmer landscape would not have had the slightest effect upon me. I was confined to a small dark room, where I was to spend six weeks of utter gloom.

When the first really bad part of the illness had departed, I determined to work again; I was not strong enough to write for long periods, certainly not to draw, so I chose another form of expression. I had fortunately brought with me a small and inexpensive camera; I determined to use this to record some of the facets of my 'cell'. The sun reluctantly peeped into my window for about twenty minutes in the early afternoon so I decided to use this time for work. My bed, with its cage still over it, bore upon it a fine assortment of objects, which lay scattered until they were tidied up by the nurse each evening. It was the breakfast and lunch tray which first caught my attention. My meals were entirely frugal and the trays reflected this frugality in a Buffet-like way. But it was only possible, due to the light, to use the tea tray which appeared at the same time as the sun, its contents certainly, less glamorous. Two pieces of dry bread and jam and a cup of tea without milk! Real prison fare. I began taking a series of photographs of this tray from different angles, my sunglasses, the white plate with a knife angled across it, and the cup and saucer. Then I would spend the rest of the afternoon sending off the film to be developed.

I enjoyed unloading the dry roll of film and fixing it firmly with the sticky paper which appeared so dutifully on the last strip. It was a reverse process to the bandaging of my feet, about an hour later, when the small, complacent, blue packages would be torn apart and the white cotton rolls wound round my ankles. I could not help comparing these two not so dissimilar sized rolls, which executed such different tasks. One roll, the slim, hard film one, enclosed, in a second of time, something stilled and caught for ever. The other one, so neatly wrapped in blue, was the protector of a living organism, the seal which hid the magic healing of ulcers and sores. The bandage was part of the development of life, re-birth; the film was, when developed, a link with the past. Two such entirely different duties were both of importance to me in that small cell-like ward.

My camera was a simple Kodak, with just a press button. It had no time exposure. But I did fortunately have with me a close-up lens so that I could take pictures within three feet.

I found great beauty in the simple objects upon that tray. They certainly meant little to me as nourishment; often I did not even eat the food set before me, so ill did I feel. But constantly I felt their 'power' and their significance, and realised, perhaps for the first time, that life held more than I expected. I owe part of my recovery to that small camera, which interpreted my signs for me and opened up a whole new world.

CHAPTER SEVEN

I WAS WARNED that I must limit my standing when I left hospital, but it would not be true to say that I took my next job entirely on these grounds, though I may have kidded myself that it was so at the time. Standing plays an important and ceremonial part in the life of an expert taxi driver. I wanted adventure, with the minimum strain on my legs and enough cash coming in to continue painting and writing. A flush of hope was born in that jaundiced ward as I spent a week of preparation converting, through the correct postal channels, my little crimson Standard 8 into a fully qualified and licensed country taxi. I dispatched cards left, right and centre to local garages, hospitals, schools, vicarages and large houses near my cottage on the Berkshire Downs. By the time I had flooded the Berkshire countryside with two hundred announcement cards, I foresaw the future in truly rosy terms. A small start in the district, perhaps a few months, then a chain of taxis stretching far across the Berkshire Downs, into the Thames Valley, down into Sussex via Petworth and up into the West Country, linking Bristol and Bath in a perfect unison of automation. Linked to the same Company would be the Scottish Highlands after I had crushed all the taxi business in the Lowlands. The Outer Hebrides, and some of those fiercer derelict islands, would automatically be enmeshed by my network, and a charter boat chain would link up the sea with my land activities. As I stuck the last stamp to the last card, I sealed my future prosperity, a nation-wide fleet of taxis inter-communicated from North to South, East to West, bearing my personal insignia. I had not decided upon the personal emblem (might it be a pendant flag?) which would make my nation-wide fleet as quickly recognisable as the Queen's head on a coin. This was a matter I could thrash out with a leading publicity agent, someone like Colman,

Prentice and Varley, or Walter Thomson's, when I was less busy. They, in conjunction with Victor Stiebl, would quickly resolve the dress of my drivers, perhaps changing the colour of the cloth with the district: a gorse yellow for the Highlands, a misty blue for the Lowlands, and perhaps a dignified grey for the Berkshire area. Bright scarlet would bring the necessary glow to the Midlands.

My family were eagerly awaiting (well at any rate, were awaiting) my return, convinced that I should at last be forced into practising a more practical aspect of art and would train as a commercial artist. 'Taxis Unlimited' was my resolute, if rash, answer to this.

My cottage on the Berkshire Downs, not far from where my father lived, did not burst with enthusiasm on my return. No sooner had I unlocked the stable-type door to the front parlour than I was met by three unpaid rating requests, eight magnificently out-dated bills, and seven black kittens. Their enthusiasm might be conceded, but as none of them was born when I left for hospital, I fear their pleasure was merely an expression of their natural high spirits. Maybe the three who had nested in my radiogram, on top of my Kathleen Ferrier records, had lyrically musical tendencies. It certainly scared them out of their wits when Orson Welles sumptuously read Walt Whitman's 'Leaves of Grass' from the very heart of the radiogram on the night of my return. (By the time Orson Welles had finished, I realised that if by any chance the taxi business should flounder, away in the Hebrides or somewhere, I should of course go and nurse sick soldiers, in between milking cows and lambing lambs.)

I remember the very first call with much delight. A local vicar rang one morning and asked if I would take his wife and daughter to a church some distance away. When I arrived to pick them up, I could see that they were disappointed in the appearance of my taxi. I am sure they had expected a large black Daimler with a glass partition. Instead, there was my little crimson Standard 8 which needed the front seats pushing forward to allow access into the back. I had forgotten to take out my shooting stick which was lying in the back; poor Mrs. Vicar nearly went headlong. I decided to take a shilling off their fare for this error of judgement.

It was a strange experience driving along and being 'talked through'. I longed to put them straight on one or two matters which they were discussing. Then suddenly little Miss Vicar said to her mama, "Oh, mama, I've forgotten the boiled sweets.' I only just resisted saying, "Shall I turn back for them?" Miss Vicar continued in her sad little voice, "I left the boiled sweets upon the mantelshelf." (She managed to pronounce 'boiled' as 'boyyelld' but it had none of the Celtic beauty which my phonetic spelling gives it.) It was indeed a sad situation. Five miles from home, on a Sunday morn, without boyyelld sweets. What were we to do? "Never worry, dear," replied her mama, "we'll send Aunt Maud some barley sugar on Monday." Poor Aunt Maud I thought, and put my foot down hard on the accelerator.

The taxi business began to prosper. I bought for fifty pounds a handsome 1930 Daimler *with* a glass partition and an exquisite silver vase for flowers. It was a magnificent car and of course really did look like a taxi. I managed to get some painting done in between calls, but as the business prospered, so my leisure time became scarcer and scarcer. I found myself greatly in demand. I had a switch system put through on my telephone, to the other half of the cottage, where I had installed a young married couple in exchange for 'doing for me' and looking after the garden. If I supped out, I left instructions to be called by Pam if the fare was more than fifteen shillings. I remember a very stuck-up dinner party in a large house nearby; I was one of the party and I was finely dressed in a dinner jacket. At the end of the meat course the butler approached me and whispered, "There's a message for you, sir—it's a pound." I excused myself from my hostess, murmuring something about the water system at the cottage needing attention, leapt into my taxi, earned a pound and returned in time for the cheese course.

Living a few villages from me was an enchanting old lady who had recently bought two of my landscapes and had patronised the taxi for long journeys on several occasions. She rang one day and asked if I would taxi her about eighty miles to her sister's house, where she was lunching; and she asked me to join her for lunch. This was a fine piece of patronage; a really long drive and lunch into the bargain. I put on my one good suit, picked a flower for my buttonhole, and polished the Daimler.

It was a fine summer day when we set off for Wiltshire. We arrived just in time for lunch at a picture-book Georgian house. My patroness's sister was a dignified member of the older generation, still surrounded by servants and a pre-war standard of living. Her hair was completely white. She must have been well into her eighties and she had a companion not much younger who shared the house with her. I had agreed with my friend not to mention the taxi business; we both thought this more tactful considering her age and opinions. I was introduced as a young painter working on the Berkshire Downs; no more was said. The Daimler certainly looked very much in keeping with the setting, proudly parked outside the front door. We lunched extremely well and then spent a delightful afternoon tottering round the garden. At tea time it began to rain, and it was coming down hard by the time we had to leave.

We had just climbed into the car and were saying further farewells when I decided to wind up the window against the rain. I had quite forgotten that my windows were plastered with taxi notices, beautifully and specially designed to attract attention, I was not looking at the window as I wound it up, but when I did, I was suddenly confronted by the backs of the notices, and between the gaps I saw a pair of distorted faces, which reminded me of those grotesque funfair mirror reflections. I thought the companion was going to have a fit. I drove off, a little like a scene in a Charlie Chaplin film, leaving the two astonished octogenarians gazing after us. I could almost hear the one saying to the other, "Emily, do you know we have just been entertaining

a taxi driver? What shall we do? A taxi driver! My dear, what is
the world coming to?" They would probably have died, right
there in the drive, if they had seen the left-hand notice which
proclaimed, 'If you can pay, I'll take you on your way'. And
there were plenty more wound down at the back, which sang of
'A day by the sea, for a very small fee', 'The further you go, the
less money you blow'. And a large one: 'TAXEE, THAT'S ME.'

I was beginning to feel fit again and the driving certainly saved
my legs from the constant standing which art teaching had neces-
sitated. Soon I should be ready for the final operation and, I
hoped, a teaching post in an art school.

My father has always backed me in my ambition to paint and
write. He has, like many fathers of aspiring artists, had moments
of deep concern; he has seen me doing all kinds of jobs to keep
ticking, everything from a lavatory attendant at the Festival
Gardens to art therapy on the back wards of a large London
mental hospital. But he has always given me his full support and
encouragement. At this time, the taxi period, he was greatly
concerned about my health, and felt it was time I settled to earn-
ing a more regular income from my art. He knew nothing about
my present occupation. In fact, he did not know that I had left
hospital after the jaundice attack; he was, I am sure, confidently
awaiting a phone call from his Prodigal Son announcing enrol-
ment in a commercial art studio, and a happy and prosperous life
henceforth. The story I relate I heard from a friend a few days
after it occurred.

My father was out shooting. He had just delighted himself by
getting a 'left and right'. "Good shot, Rossiter!" said a voice nearby, "you're in fine form today." There was a pause and my
father's neighbour on the shoot added, "Quite a coincidence, a
taxi starting up in the district run by a Rossiter. It's an unusual
name". My father fired again, hit another pheasant, winged a
second, and did a 'double take'. "My God—my son must be out
of hospital!"

That evening the telephone rang. My cottage was three miles

from my father's house; when I picked up the receiver I was convinced that this was not the distance. During the roar which exploded into the little parlour sitting-room, I gathered that I had not been sent to Eton to learn to drive a taxi, and that I was completely irresponsible, thoughtless and a waster. Quietly I tried to explain my motives, about my legs, how well the taxi was doing, and how much writing and painting I was doing. But I soon found I was talking to myself. The receiver at the other end had been slammed down. I went into the kitchen to prepare the cats' food. I had a family of seven to support.

About a fortnight later the telephone rang about 7 a.m. An unusually early call, I thought. It was my step-mother; would I come over and take my father to the station; his car had gone wrong. My father's voice took over the receiver; I was to come quickly, he must catch the 7.45, a most important board meeting.

"Well," I said, "all my drivers are off at the moment, I shall have to do the job myself. My drivers don't report until . . ."

There was an explosion which nearly fused the telephone. I realised I had overstepped the mark. "I'll be along," I said, "I'll do the job myself." Our journey to the station was an entirely silent one. As my father got out of the taxi he murmured something about sending the money along.

"I'm sorry," I said, "but the one thing I have been told, in the taxi business, is never to allow tick." My father solemnly handed me a note; I noticed there was no tip.

From that moment my taxi seemed to be accepted in the family, if not entirely agreed with.

But the end of my taxi career came in another way. I was doing the hospital service twice a week, taking elderly patients to hospital and then returning them home. Although I received less per mile for this type of work, it was an assured income, as my bookings were made a week ahead. I felt too that I was providing help to a worthy and useful service.

One morning I went to my own doctor to pick up an elderly patient, For the past few days I had been feeling very unwell, although I had not admitted it to anyone. As soon as I entered the doctor's surgery he said, "You don't look at all well. Sit down and let's take your temperature." The thermometer soon betrayed my state, a second attack of jaundice; and I was packed off to the local nursing home, seething with rage, my taxi tucked away in the village garage. I was down the snake again, right down its tail, in a nursing home that boasted smug green lawns, with tottering old ladies, wearing green eyeshades, perambulating them. Some of them even had parasols. I lay back in bed to work out the next move. Suddenly I felt entirely exhausted by the efforts of the past few months. Tears came to my eyes and I found myself weeping bitterly. I noticed the blue-white drops drizzling down on to my hands. I had not cried like that for years. I felt wretched, beaten and unable to resist any more. Sister came in, all white and blue, stiffly starched. I felt trapped. She obviously saw that I was very upset and tactfully withdrew. The room was darkening, the bed table bare, the windows closed, the curtains were an appalling colour, the door slightly peeling. The room had no compensations. I really had slid on the very longest snake.

And so came the end of my cottage days, by way of the second dose of jaundice and the further leg operation. But I really cannot go on to my move to Somerset without dallying for a short time over that sixteenth-century rose-and-honeysuckle-covered cottage which was my home, along with several large families of black kittens, for about three years.

I chose to be remote and rose-covered, a recluse. But as it turned out, I was neither remote nor a recluse, and only the cottage was rose-covered. You entered the parlour sitting-room via a stable-type door, shiny black outside and white on the inside. The room had the perpetual mustiness of age, was cloaked in half-darkness, and it housed my collection of books, a radiogram, three armchairs purchased for their comfort rather than their elegance, and a flurry of kittens. At the drop of a hat they fell out of cupboards, crannies and bookshelves in a scamper of delight. A small dining alcove looked out of the far end of the room on to a lawn which I regularly forgot to mow. Elms surrounded us on all sides and a glory of growth entangled itself round their bases, so that by the end of the summer I was encircled by a jungle which would have delighted the eye of Douanier Rousseau. Upstairs, if you did not remember to bend your head, you saw stars. But if you took the necessary precaution you saw an old-world cottage bedroom which needed only four books to parallel the bed to the floor.

During the years at Noakes Hill Cottage I became, somehow, involved with the village cricket club and fête committee, and over long trestle tables was drawn into battles which put to shame the wrangles of City and Wall Street boards. Our great drama always arose around fête month. It centred on £8 and whether we should insure against rain or not. By my third year of office as secretary, I understood clearly that not even Mr. Clore or Mr. Cotton could have convinced the Committee of the wisdom of insurance. "I don't believe in Insurance and all that," was Fred's annual comment, "I just doesn't believe in it. The Insurance bloke always wins, you mark my words. . . ."

The point, not that Insurance Companies 'always wins', but that we should not lose a large sum, never worked itself into Fred's head. Of course, a majority vote would have won the day and invested the eight pounds wisely and solidly against rain, storm and tempest; and a further twopence would probably have insured the large trestle table against the fierce onslaught of Fred's fist as he brought it down in crashing emphasis, "I doesn't believe in Insurance, that's final". But matters were not resolved in that democratic way. Perhaps this was not surprising in a village founded in the way ours had been. The standard of our cricket team would not have come up to the skill of an Australian touring side, but we did share a distinction in common with this mighty outpost of the Commonwealth: both our communities had been founded by ex-convicts. A hundred years or so before, all the old poachers (and the young ones), all the bigamists, thieves, lechers and sinners in general, had settled in our village after, presumably, turning the treadmill countless times in Reading Gaol.

It was not a fact forgotten by neighbouring villages. It was at times almost impossible to arrange cricket fixtures. Country folk have long memories. Whether it was expected that our team would be handicapped by a ball on a chain round their ankles, or whether it was mere snobbism, I never found out. We certainly enjoyed a smaller list of fixtures than the neighbouring villages.

But any disenchantment with the past history of the village was entirely compensated by the rare enchantment of Lady Muriel Percy. She had lived in the village for many years and symbolised the best and most precious qualities which a few of the real aristocracy have inherited through generations of spacious lawns, turret towers and acceptance of high responsibility. To tell you that she cut her lawn with nail scissors, often by moonlight, as she was convinced that this was the treatment grass preferred, only gives a hint of her deeply felt love of nature and particular charm. While shopping once in Reading she was heard to murmur, "The sun is in, of course it would be, it's half-day closing".

She was tall and aristocratically distinguished in appearance, blending perfectly with her worn tweeds. Her voice was deep and beautiful and I once listened, fascinated, to a two-hour discourse on St. Paul from her, over a cup of cocoa; she admired St. Paul fervently.

I once asked her to supper. "Well that's very kind of you, Anthony, most kind I must say, but I do think it's a most extraordinary habit eating other people's food. It seems so unfair. Now perhaps I could bring my own cereals . . ."

So she supped at my cottage, bringing with her her own large packet of cornflakes and her special brand of intelligence and ironical wit.

Part 2

CHAPTER ONE

I SOLD MY cottage, my kittens and my overgrown garden in
Berkshire, and went for interview at a famous school near Glastonbury. I drew near. I sighted a lolloping farmer-like figure,
back view, white cricket boots slung round its shoulders, with a
head the shape of the sun. It was lolloping right into that element,
silhouetted dark against the orange glow.

I stopped to give it a lift. It talked to me of cricket, the school,
cider and many matters of much importance, and informed me
how to handle my interview. We exchanged names. It was my
first meeting with Robert Bolt, who was, at that time, head of
the English Department at Millfield School, where I was going
for interview. He taught English, as only a genius can, from an
upturned boat in an old Nissen hut.

I was appointed to the post. Bob and I became close friends
and neighbours, and a year later he scored his first great success
in the theatre with *Flowering Cherry*, gave my wife away at our
wedding and lent us a hundred pounds to get married on.

I began re-organising the art department in a greenhouse
which allowed the pupils to watch their plants blooming, inch
by inch, as they drew. It was really a unique and delightful
experience.

Again my legs went wrong. I travelled to London, was
operated upon, and returned to Somerset intent upon aiding
the new flow of blood in my legs, which I did by stumping
round the orchards and lanes. I sensed a link between the juice
which my foot on occasion crushed out of an apple, during these
orchard rambles, and the new life forces within my legs.

I stayed with Jane and David Cory-Wright in their enchanting
house, set in an orchard, close to Glastonbury Tor; their care and
kindness were to change the whole direction of my life drama-

5*

tically during the next few months. They were the hinges to the closed doors of the future. If I write that their hospitality was not quite matched by the sterilising power of Jane's old kitchen iron, which pressed my dressings late each evening, I am both stating a fact and my profound appreciation of its intent. Charms, as the ancients knew so well, work their own peculiar way.

I owe my wife to that old charming iron.

I travelled again to London for permission to work standing, when the two weeks recuperation had elapsed. My heart filled in the bare winter fields with posies of flowers, as the train dashed towards Paddington. The pain in my left leg was the natural outcome, I persuaded myself, of the recent operation. Or was probably psychosomatic.

A nurse unwound the dressings in Outpatients. We both saw the cause of the trouble, its results stained ochre and crimson and woven into the gauze. Our reactions were different. She cool and calm, dismissed the erring dressing into a bin, in the way she would discard a rotten tomato in the kitchen; then she stood, arms behind her back, waiting for instructions. The surgeon's sentence was short. "You'll have to stay, I'm afraid." But for me, at that moment, it was a sentence of death.

I was allowed a few minutes to collect some necessary articles from the hospital shop, the usual array, soap, flannel, toothbrush, lavender talcum-powder, a razor, all the toilet articles which would soon become stickily associated in the bedside locker and soften the hairbrush bristles overnight. I had not even one book with me.

Disconsolately, with a limp as much in my heart as my leg, I made my way to the ward. Back to square one yet again.

I knew only too well what I should find in the ward. Wards have one quality in common with the Roman Catholic faith. Their dogma and pattern are the same the world over. The lockers, the towels, the envelope-folded beds, the disconsolate pairs of wireless headphones, the reading lights which imme-diately suggest that you will have time to read the whole of

Shakespeare's works before you die; the temperature chart, the bed tray, the wheels, well there they were all over again. It takes time to discover the poetry within these objects; it does not hit you straight away as you enter; certainly not in the frame of mind in which I found myself on that dark wintry evening.

But in this ward I found the unexpected. Through the open door I saw, by the bare brown locker, the most beautiful nurse in the world. She was the Archangel Gabriel herself. She wore a Swiss watch (or so it seemed) upside down on her bib: it had a neat red cross inscribed upon it. When she spoke, her charming accent further persuaded me that this angel of mercy had bloomed amongst the wild flowers of the Alps, her childhood days marked by the chimes of a cuckoo clock and her cheeks rouged in red by the snow. But my geography proved inaccurate; this beautiful girl had bloomed amongst the tulip fields of Holland, her childhood punctuated by guttural German voices and machine-gun fire.

Certainly I added charm to my simmering anger as I helped her sort out my name, address, age, religion, number of teeth, temperature and wide interests. I readily held out my arm for the pulse take, and with no surprise registered the rise in my temperature, as the nurse neatly marked the effects she had had upon me on the chart.

I had never really overcome my shyness with girls, due in some measure to my illness in Greece, and this shyness increased in proportion to the attraction of the girl. I had developed, in the prideful way man does, a technique which gave the outside world the impression that my love affairs were legion and no film hero would get a look in—essentially a protective device to compensate for my lack of success. I left the art school with the reputation of a Don Juan. Add to this a face (particularly with a cigar in it) and a figure which suggest that I have just come from an expansive luncheon at the Savoy, and you will see that the picture of me, to the outside world, differs somewhat from the real and complicated one. In fact, by the cold light of day, or rather in the dark recesses of night, my reputation was based on a minimal number of kisses, most of which deserve the title of 'peck'. And during the next few months I lost two fiancées, one late at night at Reading Station and another on the Sussex Downs. The latter to a farmer named, if I remember correctly, Rabbit: Paul, not Peter.

My future wife then ran me a bath.

Now I sank into the deep Victorian bath in the first flush of renewed hope. In the soothing warm water my seething anger changed into something soft and lathery. I began to sing. I sang until there was a severe rap upon the door and that charmingly accented voice said, "Please be a little quieter, Mr. Rossiter, you're disturbing all the patients." How dare patients sleep, I thought, with such beauty around. And so my mood changed, cleansed by the water and hope. While vigorously rubbing myself dry, I was already planning a return to teaching, if necessary in a wheel-chair. By the time I was back in the ward I had determined a course of action. A telephone by the bedside; the future could be straightened. The Ministry of Pensions would surely provide a wheelchair and it would then be possible to resume teaching at the first opportunity. I ate an enormous dinner and was in a happy state of mind to meet the surgeon's inspection late in the evening.

When the door of my room closed that evening, with the telephone installed by the bed, and my legs re-bandaged, I felt more than another door opening. It seemed that the windows were blown open too and that I was floating out into a world of known and unknown bliss. My mind soared into regions of pure heaven.

My wife's version of our first meeting, in that January ward at St. Thomas', is different from mine. She maintains that, having shown me my room, she returned to the Ward Sister and said,

"There's a black, unshaven and very disgruntled man in Room 16. We must give him a bath."

I certainly was very angry when I just glimpsed her, probably unshaven, and was wearing a battered old army overcoat. I had only come to London for a final leg inspection, with a return ticket to Somerset in my pocket. I had merely come for permission to resume teaching. My whole future again seemed in jeopardy; the teaching post, so recently won, seemed to be slipping through my fingers. I had already had a month's leave from teaching, at the start of the term, to allow the operations time to heal. I had promised to resume work after visiting London.

My life has never been a simple one; many of the complexities which fill it stem from my complex and irrational nature. Impulse has very often created situations which, in retrospect, belong to the world of Alice in Wonderland or Walter Mitty. So that if you move to a scene, set not far from St. Thomas' Hospital, on the bridge in St. James' Park, on which a dark, squat, gesticulating figure is verbosely discussing a thousand topics at once, hand in hand with a pretty nurse, early in February 1957, you will begin to understand the pattern of the rest of the year. The fact that this particular pretty nurse did not fully understand English, nor my impassioned discourses on the paintings at the Tate, to where we went on this first date, did not matter. I was in love with the bridge over the pond, the beads of water on the ducks' beaks, winter, London's loneliness, myself, the Guardsmen, the paintings at the Tate, the glistening, rainswept roads and this beautiful nurse. And I tried to convey all this in a few hours.

It was a miracle to me that I was free of hospital in such a short time, out in the wintry desolation of London, and heading back for Somerset. I was allowed to walk as much as I liked, but not to stand. It is no metaphor to say that I swept my future wife off her feet. So intensely joyous did I feel, and so much did my spirits soar, that I swept all before me. There was no taxi to be found outside the Tate, so we swept on, through a deluge of rain, towards Paddington, my legs in full action, spattering Anneka with rain, she calm and composed though very damp.

In Paddington I bought two tickets, the one for myself back to Somerset, the other a return for Anneka to Chippenham. It seemed the obvious and delightful end to this day, she and I dining *à deux* on the train while it rollocked along, heading for the West Country. My romantic imagination was further increased by the warmth and comfort of the first-class carriage, in which I had grandly booked. The restaurant attendant allowed me to prop up my legs. Regally we dined, with wine and brandy, and all the time I was discoursing on the exquisite grandeur and potentialities of life; and all the time it was raining, and growing darker and darker outside, and the grey-white beads of moisture cloistered themselves over the windows, which had to be wiped to discover at which station, if any, the train had stopped. The very patterns which my hand made upon the window made me exclaim even more upon the mystery and potentialities of life, its magic and possible meaning. The smear upon the pane resembled a lake, a vast expanse of darkly brooding water seen from the air, and encircled by a myriad array of minute conifers, clustering round like gazelles drinking at an evening watering place. As the window gently steamed over again, I was reminded of mist, and I found myself explaining those paintings we had so recently seen at the Tate—particularly Turner's 'Rain, Steam and Speed'. We were enveloped in a world which he might have painted himself; here we were hurtling through the late evening, prophetically affirming the great painter's vision. However there was nothing vaporous about our dining-table, the glasses, plates, cups, and saucers nor the bottle of wine; they represented Manet, not Turner.

Our speed had been hindered by the rain and mist, so that on arrival at Chippenham we found the return connection had departed. Anneka was stranded. I had visions, at that moment, of death and disease rampaging through a ward robbed of one of its nurses. "It's all right," said Anneka comfortingly, "I'm not on duty till tomorrow afternoon." I saw death assuaged sharp at 2 p.m.

We found an exchanting small hotel for Anneka in Westbury. I assured her, after her bewildered glance at a cluster of antlers in the hall, that we were not in the Highlands but in the West Country. Her confidence seemed to return and she smiled again. As I settled the bill and the next morning's taxi, I felt like the Good Samaritan at that Biblical inn two thousand years ago; "I'll pay thee more on my return". And so we parted.

Occasionally, these days, we drive past the telephone box near Glastonbury from where I rang the next morning to see if Anneka was all right. It has a special place in our affections, for it was on that line that she first said, 'good-bye, darling'. But much was to happen, many angsts and fears reared up their troublesome heads, before finally we married at the end of the year.

The wheelchair was waiting for me in the art room at Millfield School. I was the richer by a new form of bandaging, freedom to work again, and a fine friend in the young nurse. Life was good again; the orchards would be foaming within three months, a sight to heal any sore.

I set up home in a very large room at 'The Rose and Portcullis' in Butleigh, directly above the bar. The proprietor and his wife, Arthur and Beat Pope, made me one of the family and extended help in many ways. I settled into the pattern of Somerset village life and learnt the inside rhythm from this simple pub. When my legs recovered and I was fit again, I was to experience the joys of skittles, scrumpy, and village cricket followed by bread, cheese and onions. Sometimes a table laden with pigs' trotters was spread before us after a match and we ate this country fare, washed down by ample beer and scrumpy, into the early hours of the morning. It was a simple and basic life, as near to the land as I had ever got. The pub was situated in an idyllic village just three miles from where I taught. Most evenings it rang with much laughter and coarse ribaldry, the scent of manure, cornfields and cattle nor far removed. There were giants of men with arms as thick as boughs of aged apple trees, hands steak shaped, hardened by weather and toil. There were middling men blown in from the cornfields, still ripe in years and yet furrowed with age and continuous outdoor work. There were wizened little men, who reddened easily with scrumpy, and turned from ears of corn to scarlet poppies within the hour. The hard, bare, stone floor echoed with the scrape of nailed boots; the bar glistened with spilt drink, sparkling brown. Wet or dry, the bar echoed the earthiness of generations of farmers and field workers. A white, no-collared shirt, revealing black shiny hairs, sang against these browns and ochres. And there used to pass by, each morning and evening, a man straight from the pages of Thomas Hardy, who gloried in the name of (yes it's true) Jesse Traske. I knew then that the West Country was to be my permanent home.

I began teaching from a wheelchair. My spirits were soaring, the pendulum in easy motion again. I was not allowed to stand, but could drive the car and then walk short distances. Teaching from a wheelchair was no easy matter; I had to direct the art room from this sitting position, which did not suit my active temperament. I itched to be more extrovertly active, instead of barking orders like the 'Man Who Came to Dinner'. Teaching in this manner left me exhausted emotionally but not physically. It was one of the severest tests I have known; it required the maximum of self-discipline and planned action from day to day. I had to rely on the pupils to do most of the manual jobs, which I could have done in half the time myself. The hanging of paintings, framing, drawing from the standing position, were all virtually impossible. I learnt much from this three-month trial; once again I was forced to improvise and do the best with the limited means at my disposal. If I was teaching drawing to a pupil who was standing at his easel, I had to view the group of objects from an entirely different eye level, possibly a different angle. This taught me a great deal, for I had to imagine the other viewpoint. I was therefore involved in a really creative way of drawing (or seeing), with no question of 'copying'. I would make the pupil look at the group from my angle and then return to his, correcting his work from partly imaginative assessment. I was reminded of my days in bed in Greece, when I had first sat up for an hour or so, and seen my bedtray from this position. As I had slowly slipped down, eventually to the lying position through fatigue, I had been able to note the changing aspects of the tray from many different viewpoints; it had taught me to understand the genius of one aspect of Picasso's work, the double or treble image picture. I perhaps learnt to draw (or see) while on this downward slump into the horizontal position.

It was of course a time of great frustration. I would return to my room utterly exhausted emotionally and would sleep until supper time. Then, propped up in Arthur and Beat's back parlour, I would join in the evening's entertainment, consuming more than my share of scrumpy and joining in the hilarious singing which wafted in from the bar. They were good evenings which did much to revive my tired spirits so that I was ready next morning for renewed battle.

I would sit in the bathroom, legs propped on a second chair, shaving into a looking-glass leant against the window. Beyond the glass, through the window, the foaming blossoms echoed my lathered face, white against white; I was reluctant to erase the foam from my face to reveal the dark brown below. I used to shave very slowly, savouring the double image of whiteness to the full. It was a fine start to the day. The white bath behind me seemed grey indeed against the other whitenesses.

My legs recovered. Spring finally exploded in all its splendour. The birds sang their sweetest songs once more. The corn peeped through, as green as green, oh so seriously, and before long there was the scent of hay and the glory of long summer evenings. Bob Bolt, his wife Jo and I spent many an evening in their cottage just a hundred yards below the pub. He was writing; I was painting. Life was good. I would listen as Bob read the next few pages of his play, *Flowering Cherry*, written after teaching. His voice, with its beautiful touch of northern accent, would bring his evocative theme and words right into one's mind, where they lingered long afterwards. When I saw this play, which was read to me almost page by page, in London a year or so later, I really could not hear the famous actor speak the familiar lines. I could hear only the voice of their author, as he slumped in a wicker chair before a blazing fire, surrounded by his cottage furniture, his dogs, half a dozen beer bottles, and Jo, listening quietly too.

During the next few months Anneka and I courted to a pattern of alternate weekends in Somerset, when we would dine very lavishly at a nearby club on the evening she arrived, and then would eke out the remainder of the weekend with fish and chips. But the carefree spirit which manifested itself so generously as I welcomed Anneka with outstretched arms at the quiet little Somerset station, was in fact a spirit not entirely free from care; and as the weeks passed, so my subconscious fears and uncertainties increased, strangling my thoughts and making my actions indecisive.

My legs had healed by the summer and I worked long hours in the fields painting again; I was filled with joy by the waving corn, rippling across vast acres and fading to extinction against a boundary hedgerow. It reminded me of the final effort of a wave as its last remnants of power trickle gently on to the shore. It reminded me of the ripples on a pool created by gusts of wind. But I found a distinction between these two ripplings, the one on the pond somehow finite and cold, the one over a cornfield immeasurably magnificent and yet possessing an echo of eternal sadness.

It was such a mood which swept over me when I waved good-bye to Anneka at the station at the close of one of our weekends. I was filled with a poignant sadness, and yet felt relief that I was alone again, free of responsibilities and decisions. And so my indecisiveness grew; until it became the basis of a psychosomatic illness, which is worth relating, both as proof of the power of the subconscious, and for the important part it plays in this story.

As autumn approached, so my gaiety disappeared; not only did my mood echo this nostalgic season, but also I found that I desired only to sleep. As soon as my teaching was done for the day, I would return to my pub room and sleep until the next morning. As the weeks passed, the more I slept. I just could not understand it; I was perfectly fit, the legs not troubling me very much, and yet all I wished to do was sleep.

Then one evening Bob Bolt explained (with the aid of a bottle of whisky) the workings of the subconscious to me. It was the submerged portion of the iceberg which did the damage to a ship, not the glittering upper formation. I was strangled by a fear of marriage and the ensuing responsibilities. After a few hours, my subconscious was delightfully submerged in whisky, and I was again a man of action.

Bob gave Anneka away in the Parish Church in Street. I was wearing a double-breasted blue suit, which my father had recently sent me, and which, being not entirely tailored to my figure, made me feel even more inadequate than I usually do. I was constantly reminded, as I stood facing the altar, waiting for Anneka, hands perspiring alternately, that 'clothes maketh a man'. I did not feel at all like myself or like a man; and what small interior part of me did remain masculine was closely linked in a sort of reversed Oedipus complex with my father, through the suit, which prompted memories of my parents' broken marriage. The suit symbolised all the qualities which I lacked; in particular the coat lapels, so flat and manly, and the trouser turn-ups breaking with such ease and nonchalance upon my shiny black shoes, emphasised the charade in which I seemed to be acting. The iceberg was chilling my spiritual emotions, although it never froze the tiny beads of perspiration glistening in the palms of my hands.

When the photographs appeared a few days later, I clearly saw my fears permanently recorded in black and white. If I add that it rained during the whole ceremony, and even harder while we were being photographed, it gives an accurate picture of that eventful and important day.

But the sun, both literally and metaphorically, shone forth when we arrived back at 'The Rose and Portcullis', where we held the reception. Crammed into the front bar were tables laid with white cloths and loaded with a Sassoonian feast of hams, pigs' trotters, bread and cheese and onions; limitless beer and stronger fare were near at hand. The sun crept in through a coloured window, staining a corner of the table in violent yellow, green and crimson. I was suddenly filled entirely with delight; I noticed the rich brown bottles of ale singing their particular golden earthy song, as the sun blessed them for a moment. The room was full of hope and cheer and love. As the party came to an end, and Anneka and I climbed into my army van to drive to our honeymoon in Porlock, I felt a man again.

We spent three days at a charming small hotel in Porlock; it was three days before Christmas. The sea sparkled grey blue below us as we walked vigorously over the cliffs, through bare winter woods. They were entirely perfect days. We returned to spend our first married Christmas with Bob and his family. Our home was still my large room at the pub. Poor Anneka had to face Rabelaisian jokes as we passed through the bar to get to the room. No sooner did I appear in the bar than I was greeted with music hall sallies such as, "Ahh, sir, 'ee do look tirred, reel worn out. Don't 'e, Fred?" It was obvious that we must find our own home quickly. My happy, carefree bachelor days were past. It would be the Saloon Bar in the future.

Fortune favoured us. A few days after Christmas we found a four-roomed gardener's cottage overlooking Wells. It belonged to a large Victorian house which was owned by a family who had, in the most lovely fashion, resisted the times of change. The house, in decoration, mood and spirit, had stopped still in 1910. We were to become close friends of the Jenkins family and they were to help us in many ways during our stay there, particularly when the pendulum swung too high.

The cottage had no electricity; it was gas lit. It had a miraculous view over Wells, stretching away to the Tor at Glastonbury. It would be difficult to better that view. As there was a high wall outside the downstairs room, we made our sitting room upstairs and thus gained full possession of the view. We scrubbed, decorated and polished our four rooms, our first home. Within a week there were arrangements of flowers straight from the Dutch seventeenth century. Our home sparkled and shone with Vermeeresque perfection. There was only one snag! the bath. This was a primitive affair. Standing at one end was a vast copper urn which was filled with water by a hosepipe from the one tap. The urn perched over the bath, seated on a huge gas ring. We filled the urn, lit the gas, prayed silently and waited an hour. By this time the room was hysterically full of steam and we groped about to turn off the gas. We were to learn very speedily that to run the boiling water into the bath, before filling it with cold, was a fatal mistake. No sooner had you sat down, the urn end, than you were standing up again. And not sitting comfortably again for quite a few days. Fortunately for Anneka, and unfortunately for me, this was my discovery during the first bath I took. I never made that mistake again. And so we settled, almost comfortably, down to the first few months of married life. I was still teaching five and a half days a week, which was a great strain; for suddenly I was filled with a myriad ideas and working at my painting and writing every possible moment. Marriage, and the security of my first real home since childhood, had unleashed the enormous energies struggling within me.

I have purposely, at certain points in this story, described in some detail, day-to-day life and its trivialities. For everything, in a pendulum painter's life, is of importance; the apple blossoms, the ochre sienna scar on the inside of a bath, the bath plug itself, shaving soap, ripe corn, a battered gate, a winter hedgerow, two pipes gossiping on an ashtray, a nurse's veil, worn shoes, flowing streams, wastepaper baskets, deep humour, love, tears, laughter, ink marks on paper and the blue-grey smoke of a cigarette, a catch gloriously caught in the slips, white trousers against green grass—any of these—and a million other symbols and signs can swing the pendulum into regions of sheer bliss. Nothing is too trivial to record. For a person of my particular talents it is necessary to try and communicate these elated and ecstatic moments to other people. There is an inward bursting, which at times knows no bounds; the world is charged with magic; I am sure it is a parallel sensation to the taking of mescalin or the first stages of mystical experience. For a moment there is a oneness and knowingness which exceeds the bounds of normal thought processes. Richard Church described beautifully, in his autobiography *Over the Bridge*, a sensation he sometimes experiences; the essence of his experience is one of floating. I know no better word to describe the start of the high swing of the pendulum. You float out of yourself away into uncharted realms.

Recently my wife laid an old pair of shoes on my studio table, as a reminder that they needed repairing. Near them she laid some white flowers, ready for arranging and putting in the house. When I entered the studio I was immediately delighted by this group; there was no question of taking the shoes to be repaired. The shoes were just touching at the toes, kissing very gently, the flowers sprawled across singing another kind of song. I immediately set to work on this composition. As I worked, the flowers, in the warmth of the studio, began to wither. By the end of the composition it was 'Kissing Shoes and Dying Flowers' and I had spent two days of exhilaration in the presence of these contrasting objects. They had dominated those two days, the shoes so peacefully kissing, the flowers dying sadly behind them. This, I think, illustrates the problems that confront an artist: my shoes were not mended for some weeks and I was reduced to wearing one pair. The shoes in my studio became my subject matter and inspiration for the next month. Constantly this is happening with pots and pans, baskets, boxes and bric-a-brac; often I cannot empty my wastepaper basket, so fascinated and excited am I by it. It cannot be altered until I have 'worried it out of my system'.

Obviously if one lives one's life on this high emotional plane, there must be at times a considerable swing down. And when this does come, it is true hell.

Blossom foaming; in its presence I feel a 'lit-upness', not surprisingly; similarly with ripe swaying corn. The incessant rhythms of the hedgerows swing and dance in my mind, they streak through my brain, down my neck, tingle my spine and stream out of my hands so that when I come to draw, it is almost an intuitive and unreckonablewith act. I relive that shrieking hedgerow right through the tips of my fingers. The drawing spills on to the paper until my appetite for that sight and splendour are satisfied. I feel a hunger, a greed and a deep compulsion to work. Ditches, rhythmic broken gates, bric-a-brac on the studio floor, my streamlike desk, blotting paper, upright bottles, a thousand sights a day burst me into song and ecstasy. The day is not long enough to embrace fully the sights I see and love.

All objects to me, almost without exception, possess human characteristics. An upright bottle is proud, greedy, perhaps pompous, a cricket bat aristocratic and fine, an armchair deeply wise, a saucepan sure and contemplative. As I work I converse with these objects, learning from their wisdom, sadness, dignity and splendour. The flow and rhythms linking objects catch my eye; I am fascinated by the continuous link between a battered gate and an old bucket lying in a ditch. Unity is everywhere, there is a oneness, the fusion which we all desire so deeply in our daily lives. A oneness, a lit-upness, a splendour, an eternal song. As I am writing some keys are hanging from a rack, a neat row of metal keys. They are sad, forlorn, unwanted, and that is how I should paint them; but even in their forlornness there is a deep song, possessing the quality of sadness and beauty which one finds in a Negro spiritual.

I had just finished writing this paragraph when I had to go to the garage to fetch a book from the car. My eye was caught by the stone wall which separates the coalshed from the garage. It is a wall not quite reaching to the ceiling, with a sturdy beam across its top. On it were a chance collection of objects which so delighted me that I feel compelled to mention them, for once again I found song in the most casual of corners, at the most unexpected moment. The beam stretches twenty feet across the stones, some five feet above the floor. On it are some of the rubbish which my wife has recently thrown out; pale pink flower pot; a sagging sack, overlapping the beam and linking it to an old ironing-board, just peeping over the top; a grey-green upright bottle, dead centre; a horseshoe linking this to a red box; behind this box two rotting timbers, worm-eaten; a piece of hardboard links this group to a sienna brown box, perfectly rectangular, and on this is perched a pale honey coloured (oh so thin) fruit basket. And on the right, in the corner, is a dull red sackcloth, quiet and humble. The whole group is static, Chardin-like in simplicity and grandeur. I am hypnotised by it, and when my writing is finished for the day, I shall paint from it. I am only just able to drag myself away and write in the studio.

A few days after I had been so much delighted by the array of objects which had surfaced in the garage, and had worked some drawings from them, and just when life seemed so full of harmonies, both my writing and my painting were suddenly, and frighteningly, blocked. I was unable to complete this chapter and spent fruitless hours tearing quarter-filled pages to pieces in despair. Outside, it was a gloriously fine summer evening, the sky Turneresquely beautiful. But none of this fiery, eternal spirit entered into me as I gazed disconsolately out of the window. I decided to take the car out and seek joy in different trees and gates and hedgerows. The ones set so still before me, outside the studio window, had no significance.

I find driving through the countryside to be like reading some fascinating book or watching an imaginatively constructed film, the constant change of scene setting my imagination going; my thoughts and dreams are endless; I write most of my letters as I drive along, plan the next day's work, reassemble partly lost ideas, invent fresh stories and new situations. At times it is a truly Walter Mitty journey.

This particular evening, as I drove along, the magnificent sky and darkening hedgerows did little to change my mood. It seemed that I was set for a real and vicious swing, away from all that I usually loved. Quite suddenly, on a bend in the road, I saw a bright red notice board with a large white arrow pointing to the right. Somehow it was exactly right. It was a well balanced and planned sign, set firmly in position. It had a certainty and purpose. Its intention, to guide unwary drivers safely round the corner, pleased me. It had a touch of humour too, tempting me for a moment not to turn the corner, but to make straight for the signboard and fly headlong through it, a dog through the white circus hoop.

I looked down at my wristwatch. My wrist was bare; the watch was in my pocket. But in its place was a wonderfully pale strip where the sun had not touched my arm. Quite suddenly, these sights, the neat white strap mark and the white arrow peeping out of the hedgerow, pushed the pendulum. It began to swing to a faster and more melodious rhythm. I was happy again.

CHAPTER TWO

OUR COTTAGE LIFE was simple. During that first year of marriage, I was able, despite the heavy teaching post, to do a great deal of other work. I was bursting with ideas and spent almost every free moment working in my studio, in the orchards and lanes and in the fields. I vividly remember that winter, when I painted darkly brooding trees silhouetted against late evening skies, and decaying walls spread with frost and snow. One of these walls possessed a noble gesture in its decline, which reminded me of a man I had seen dying in hospital, whose dignity had cloaked his frail, worn body in heroic form. The nobility of this wall spoke to me in terms that Rembrandt often does when revealing the inner powers of man. A sprinkling of snow, one morning, covered its top, adding a poignant sadness to its mood; and then I sensed the desolation and depths of suffering which old age and decay often know so intimately. The sprinkling of snow was the thin patch of white hair on a dying man, and the sharply pointing, battered gate, close by, was a signpost directing its neighbour wall to the tomb. 'On, on, on,' it seemed to say on that particular day. But a month later the gate, a little more tilted to the ground, spoke clearly and sharply with a more finite message; 'down, down, down, down you go'.

As I walked slowly back to the cottage, I could not discard the message of the gate and wall. Lying in the bath, bringing warmth back into my body which had caught some of the chill of that winter scene, I noticed the rust mark just above the plug hole. It sang in a bright sienna way, rich and impertinent, against the cool tones of the water. It reminded me of the rusty piece of corrugated iron which had topped some hay close to the wall; there was the first hint of decay; there were the murmurs of approaching death; and yet, like ulcerous sores and bloody wounds, there was a visual glory to be found. Again, I remembered weeks spent in hospital, frightened and bewildered—blood and bandages, inspections and operations—and I sensed the eternal conflict of man to keep himself whole, against insuperable odds. As I dried myself down, I looked at the scars on my legs; they were white and sinewy and without meaning; they were now merely decorations, neat patterns and dents, like seams on women's dresses. They were my medals for all I had been through, and as far removed from the fire of action as those round, sovereign medallions which hang so complacently from a soldier's breast.

Our cottage had just four living rooms; the bathroom was made from an outhouse leading off the kitchen. The four rooms which comprised the house were two up, two down. My studio was upstairs opposite the sitting room. There was a vivid contrast between the calm order and charm of the sitting room, with its black Victorian fireplace flanked by two shelves filled with books, and my studio. This room bore witness to the expressive side of my nature, and drawings of gesticulating winter hedgerows were diary recordings of my day-to-day discoveries in nature, vital remembrances of ecstatic moments. On occasions, during that winter, the sun would burst into that room, obscuring the drawings, robbing them of their meaning and intensity. It would select a large, clean, tightly-stretched piece of paper and turn it into a vast virgin expanse of whiteness, wholly desirable, and reminiscent of a nurse's stiffly starched white apron. The sun made a sign to the paper, and the paper primed me to action, tempting my passionate instincts; and I would pour out these emotions on to this surface, raping its virginity with signs and symbols, scrawls and dashes, which burst from within me. I sensed again the compelling powers which had stormed me in Greece.

The struggle of those weeks is perhaps best symbolised by the long, steep hill which wound up to our cottage. Often I would climb Hawker's Lane, physically tired and emotionally exhausted, late in the evening, after a day working in the fields. It was a slow climb up that lane, punctuated most of the way by smug suburban houses; these dolls' houses spoke to me of security and self-sufficiency, trim lawns reflecting trim minds; part of me longed for this peaceful pact with life, but the more urgent and compulsive part of me scorned this truce and sensed in it a compromise which no artist can afford.

But it was good to be back, past the large, friendly, white gate leading to our cottage, and to feel the rough, loose gravel beneath my feet, the tactile reminder of home ground. I would enter the cottage straight into the kitchen, and there would find two exquisite kittens, and onions hanging from the wall, looped in a solemn chain, and flowers gracefully arranged in a lustre tea-pot. The stripped wood table spoke with dignity and simplicity, and with that special distinction which is, in its way, peculiar to the peasant and the aristocrat.

In the early spring, roots and branches sang joyfully, flaming their way upwards and outwards. I worked on a further poster for London Transport, stones and refreshed grasses which lay at the foot of a tree-clad hill; the trees were sienna, blue and umber-tinged with a hint of spring green. The scene spoke ecstatically of hope for the future, renewed life, and yet still maintained some of the desolate sadness of winter.

Halfway through the painting I needed another brush to complete the landscape. Leaving the easel supporting the painting, I sped back to the cottage. As I returned up the lane, I saw a clutter of Friesian cows admiring the painting. Although flattered by their interest, I was horrified to see one of them, the loveliest creature of the lot, put out her rough tongue and taste my work. This was going too far. Most artists have a weakness for appreciation of their work; but the normal tasting of a work of visual art depends, I am sure, more upon the eye than the tongue. Freud might argue that there is no real difference, that both actions stem from the same source. But I was in no mood to consider Freud's views, correct as they might be. I leapt over the five-bar gate, yelling (army style), and rushed towards the clutter. They turned their heads sardonically, really little impressed, and the artistic one gave a further lick. I slapped them on their backsides, which made more impression than the shouting. With little upward surges they cantered off, I suppose to discuss and 'crit' this new work of art, born in *their* field. Quickly I inspected the painting, which was almost finished. To my astonishment, the licks had unified a certain part of the ditch area, marrying the tones much more beautifully than I should have done. My heart was filled with deep affection for all bovine animals, in particular the Friesian kind. It gave me great pleasure, when the poster was published by London Transport for their Underground series, to point out to friends the part which I had not painted. Added to this pleasure was a letter from the Victoria and Albert Museum informing me that they had purchased this work for their Print Room.

Spring turned to summer; gone were the blue-black and sienna branches of winter hedgerows. Hoof marks were dried and stilled into the ground. The fresh songs of primroses faded against the yellowing corn, shooting upwards with such assurance. Winter growth is all gesticulation and effort. Summer growth is sure and complacent. The corn fields everywhere boasted certainty; they possessed aristocratic inheritance; they never, that particular summer, doubted their position or worth. Upright they stood, uncondescending to everybody and everything. Lusciously green at first, sovereign gold at their end.

To me the bundled corn was a constant source of inspiration all through the summer. I worked at a feverish pitch, day after day. The sun beat down in its fullest strength until dissuaded by storm clouds gathered white into the prussian sky. Then there was white, blue and yellow, married in a shocking fusion of colour; the sun might shoulder its way through once more, towards evening, casting lengthening shadows through the bristling stubble. The final scene, row upon row of minute golden pylons, was one of radiance, and as they stretched perspectively away into the shimmering distance, it was as if the end of the world had come in glory, fabulously freckled for all to see.

By the time summer had faded into autumn, I had learnt a little more about nature's fierce battle, and I felt increasingly the presence of myself within it. I seemed to be more and more intimately connected with it, and the gestures of cornstooks, weather-worn wearied gates and groaning orchards echoed my own emotions. Despite the emotive response of my whole being to these ecstatic signs and symbols in nature, in people, in objects, I never once sensed the dangerously high pendulum swing. It was a period possessing such potentialities that no fear of illness appeared to have room in its head. I could not sense, during that autumn, anything but a total life, a life filled by family, painting, teaching and writing. By late in July, we knew that our first child was to be born the following March, so that I felt my creative powers to be fully blessed on all fronts.

Through the nostalgic, sienna, yellow, crimson autumn, I moved away from angry, tormented cornstooks, to crumbling walls and gates poised against misty, ultramarine evening hazes. The blue distances, enveloping Wells and the villages I knew so well, turned the scene to one of mysterious unknowingness; through the haze there still remained something of the former scene, but cloaked as it was in mist and blue, it became another world; a world in which I could dream and romance, and which often reminded me of Ireland and the Celtic magic which shimmers from that island.

In winter the cascading walls were festooned in white; at first skimmed in glittering frost, then later loaded more amply with inches of snow. The scene became calm and static, like a still of a film; it scarcely seemed to breathe at all; biding its time, knowing that spring would follow with foaming orchards, primrosed hedgerows, and flaming branches.

Perhaps my last contentment and peace, before the pendulum swing, was during that December. While I painted, often high above Wells, I was filled with the peace and quiet which is expressed so profoundly by Breughel in his winter landscapes. Stretching below me was such a scene, such a basin, stilled and silenced under wintry whiteness, punctuated by small, dark shapes, perfectly ordered and balanced. It reminded me of the scene on the Berkshire downs, eleven years before, when the order of ploughed fields had seemed an arrangement of God's, supervised with a film director's precision and eye. In Berkshire it had been a positive, rich and coloured print. In Somerset, it seemed as if I was looking at a negative, which required further work to translate its positive face. The scene hinted darkly, as night closed in, of something temporary and transitory, which clear light and sun would interpret.

This hint of darkness seemed to hover in the air as January moved into February. The ecstasy of the gesticulating, yellow streaks of corn had imprinted itself crazily upon my mind; but the intense joy and liberation which I had experienced during that summer, a world of lit-upness, became filtered during the early part of the new year. The brooding desolation of a winter evening seemed to suspend my ecstasy, so that when I turned to look at one of the cornfield paintings in the sitting room, I was suddenly frightened. The wall below the sitting room screamed intensely with winter bitterness, and a green door shrieked vividly from within it, but these deep emotive cries contrasted strangely with the summer ones; I had turned from the desolate winter shapes to the cornstooks for comfort, but had found instead a state of strangulation and fear. These fears were to crystallise a few months later.

And so the contentment which December had brought to me changed to panic; it was a subtle change and one which I certainly did not detect. It was not a 'running away' type of panic; rather it was the reverse. I threw myself again totally into work and thus started the headlong spiral journey from whose spin I could not extricate myself without help. My work was a desperate attempt to fob off the ever-increasing panic within me.

While I worked at fevered pitch, there was besides the initial state of luminous bliss, a keen whisper in my ears of darker and different matters. The winter wind spoke strange messages and occasionally, just for an instant, I was reminded of those far-off days in Greece. The whirling spiral which engulfed me during those three months, from January to March, vibrated with echoes of thirty-three years of living and experiencing, all funnelled at times into one crammed and bursting hour. But I was not once warned by any of these memories; rather they gathered in with the recent ones, clustering for attention, bound together fiercely as strands of corn are in a stook. An endless flow of light seemed to flood the landscape, the very room in which I worked, and faces appeared lit from within. I was filled with deep compassion for all humanity, an emotion prompted by pity but demanding action to turn it from a negative response to a positive one. This compulsive sensation grew in intensity as spring began to stir, and as I sensed the sap rising in the trees, so I felt the life force within me bursting for release, a force which would ignite all I touched, turning suffering to joyous expectation.

Since marriage I had again become acutely aware of the rhythmic flow of all around me, noting its subtle changes from day to day, from the stillness of winter to the stirrings of early spring. It had been a period of intense work, begun in the January of our marriage through to the swelling trees and hedgerows of March, into the foaming orchards of May and on to the soft sproutings of early corn. Then on to the full yellow burst of fields shimmering in the evening light, right into the cutting and flaying, the tormented stooking. Summer had passed into autumn and autumn into winter. I had wished for an eternity of time to say what I could of these changing seasons. An artist is a compulsive creature, he will create 'come what may'; this is not to say that what he creates will be fine or lasting, but in the act of creation he will be fulfilling himself and unravelling certain strands.

Although the urgency of my work hammered away during those months, demanding a hearing, and despite the sinister whispers on a windy wintry day, neither my wife nor I sensed the gathering storm clouds early in March; little did we realise that the near future held such a blow to our security. All seemed so very well. Our first child was due in the middle of March and that month was filled, both literally and metaphorically, with sunshine. We sat many an afternoon in the walled garden below the sitting room, basking in the early sun, watching winter evaporate into spring.

My mind buzzed round the number three. These were my days of Trinity. I had seen three wise men talking near the Cathedral in Wells. They had turned and given me a sign of recognition, which was re-echoed later that evening when I was searching through a drawer of old objects in my studio, and had discovered just three of my old regimental buttons, three not five. This was further proof of all that was to come, three regimental buttons which when I polished them shone as bright as the night stars. Looking out of the studio window I noticed the latch was held in hole number three. And I could see three black fir trees silhouetted against the magenta night sky. When I added the stars in the sky they became multiples of three. Soon we were to be a perfect Trinity, a unit of three. It was written in the sky, in the glittering army buttons and in the flame of the third struck match which set the bowl of my pipe aglow, as I gazed through the three frames of the studio window.

I remember drawing three walls. I felt a compulsion to add two more to the original one. To perpetuate the magic around and within me, it was essential to work in threes. Just as important as not crossing the lines on the pavement or having to touch every third lamp post in a particular street. I drew bulbs spurting through the brown earth, in clusters of three.

Gates in fields were no longer barrier sentinels. With a flick of my finger I could, if I wished, whisk them open so that the fields were free. The time was approaching for all tombs to open, all men to arise, and all barriers be broken down. There was not one curse in my heart and I knew no fear

6

I drove the car to London, carrying with me bouquets of love and praise to shower upon all I met. These bouquets I showered upon my mother, artist friends and a distinguished art critic whom I met at dinner above the gallery where I was to show my paint-ings. Staying with Robert and Chris Roberts in Twickenham, I arose early in the morning and floated out of the house down to the river, flickering with the haze which stretched across its sur-face. The smooth passive passage of the water drifted into me and I wafted down the river path as cool and light as a skiff. This harmony purred within me driving back to Somerset, its tempo and power increasing more fully as I put down my foot upon the accelerator. The purr turned to a throb; the engine power was an extension to my own overcharged battery. I hit a wall; the dent to the right door was merely a symbolic mark upon my shield. I threw of my shield and left it lying in the road. Back at the cottage I went straight to my studio desk. And upon it I poured a thousand words of praise which gathered momentum with the aid of gin. And thus I slept, slumped across the desk, my head pressing hard upon the words so recently tumbled there.

Annalisa was born on the 16th March, making our unit the perfect three. The signs were working, the glory gathering. My mind would not cease working even during sleeping hours, so that I worked in my studio late into the night and then on to the early hours of the morning. I did not once sense the danger, I was too much primed with joy and glowing light. Life appeared an indestructible element. I was fused with flowers and grasses, walls and hedgerows, floating over fields and streams, sailing out into a world of eternal bliss. I could if I wished break forth the sun from behind the clouds, or pour dismal streaks of rain by merely changing my mood and countenance.

I have recently found a piece of writing which I did at this time. Looking at it now, it has all the warning of future develop-ments. But when I wrote it, I was in no condition to read deeper implications into my writings; I was 'superman', indestructible, flowing with eternal life. It is only now, some four years older

and wiser, that I can read the warning. I quote the piece of writing
to reflect the unrealised agony of the high pendulum swing,
which though so full of bliss, bore within it a future hell.

Insomnia

There is nothing sweeter than sleep, the dream of sleep
Before the candle flickers and the moths come hurtling,
I know a moment so silent that it is still, quite still;
This moment has full potency
Is not full of leisurely repose,
    Sleep of the Gods,
        the logs,
           the dogs, the door mat, just the knocker at rest.
That is what I want, a knocker to knock sleep into the door
    of my mind
And to lay it on its mat, next to the dogs, in front of
    the logs,
    Very near the Gods.

During the high pendulum swing one possesses many of the
qualities experienced under alcohol. There is a 'oneness', a love
for all, a faith in the world akin to a child's. John Custance talks of
this in his book *Wisdom, Madness and Folly*, and quotes most
aptly from some lines of Walt Whitman's. I really cannot do
better than requote these lines, for they express perfectly the
sensation one feels:

Swiftly arose and spread around me the peace
and knowledge that pass all the argument of the earth,
and I know that the hand of God is the promise of my own,
And I know that the spirit of God is the brother of my own,
And that all the men ever born are also brothers,
    and the women my sisters and lovers.
And that a kelson of the creative is love.

John Custance then continues: "It is actually a sense of communion, in the first place with God, and in the second place with all mankind, indeed with all creation. It is obviously related to the mystic sense of unity with ALL . . ."

The world sped in supersonic sequences past me. Suddenly all the bells were ringing, for the whole world and for me in particular. The age-old cathedral bells were my instrument and charge as much as the wristwatch on my arm. They understood perfectly all that I was feeling, that was their reason for breaking into chime. I was inhabiting a spiritually democratic world where orders were only given when agreed to by all. I seemed to possess the total powers of the world inside me and I felt that my flaming spirit was uniting with a billion others, and that all was shared between us. Our loves clashed cymbal-sharp above the glittering earth and sparked upwards, arrowed to the sun. And in the radiance of the sun our souls would melt into one, poured coolly back in sheets and drops of rain. Thus would the full cycle of our love return, blessing grass and hills and corn.

Everything began to flow too fast. Mathematically it had become Communion to the power of ten. I was in the realm of higher metaphysics and quite untutored in it. What was I to do? I turned to nature for the answer. I looked out of the window and saw the early morning grass laughing with pebbles of dew; but as I gazed at it, the tinkling laughter turned first to mocking tones and then with frightening speed to hysterical screams, sounds thrown back from the innermost regions of hell, echoing and reverberating like a voice imprisoned in a cave. 'God, God, God, God. . . .' This one name seared into my mind; I wanted to scream.

I picked up the telephone to ring God direct. The fact that I did not get through to God surprised me at the time. I was convinced that I had dialled G.O.D. But it was reassuring to talk with my aunt; the muddling of the numbers I felt to be part of the plan. As a devout Roman Catholic, she must, I felt sure, be involved in this religious project. It was, of course, annoying not

to speak direct with the Boss, but comforting to be in close contact. My aunt's surprise at this very early call, and its strange
content, did not really register with me. But it was a fortunate
call, for she was responsible for contacting my doctor and stem-
ming the flight of the pendulum.

After the telephone call, I calmed down. I walked round the
garden with a prayer-book in my hand. In my mind, I saw myself as a saintly monk, black cassocked, weaving my hands gently
through a rosary. I was not at that time a member of the Roman
Catholic Church, though I presumed myself to be so; not only a
member but a vitally important functionary. The giddy heights
which I reached, within a few hours, make a mockery of the
swiftest promotion known in officer ranks. By the time my doctor had arrived, with another person whom I did not recognise,
I was supremo, Christ himself, and the small luncheon party
which we held in the sitting room was a strange affair. Our faithful daily help, I remember distinctly, served us cold ham, lettuce
and fried potatoes. And all the while I ate, I was aware only of a
destiny which beckoned me, a destiny that required noble self-
sacrifice and compliance with anything that was asked of me. It
was a strangely peaceful meal, the three of us perched forward in
our chairs, with our plates upon our knees; I do not remember
much of the conversation; there were questions, I seem to remember answering these with much assurance, almost brushing
them aside as a batsman flicks a ball through the slips with a late
cut. It all seemed so pointless; surely these two men must know
who I was and what all this was about. And so our luncheon
party ended, all most amicably, and I readily agreed to my doctor's suggestion that I should go to hospital later in the afternoon.
He told me he would call back in an hour or so, giving me time
to pack a few things.

During that hour I packed almost all my belongings which had
any connection, visually and in writing, with the first pendulum
swing in Greece. I have no memory of doing this. It is interesting
that when finally I unpacked my cases in hospital, I discovered

photograph albums, diaries, drawings, books bought in Greece, even the camera which I had used there; I had surrounded myself, subconsciously, with the expressions and remembrances of that Grecian swing, rather as a mourner decorates a grave with vases of flowers.

I felt myself going to a tomb, from which I would arise triumphant on the Monday morn. It occurs to me only now that my burial was more Egyptian than Christian in style; but what did occur to me at the time was the fact that I should have to 'work like hell' while in the tomb, preparing a modern mystic manifesto for publication on the Monday morn; hence the need for my Olivetti typewriter and a pile of paper.

I might add that the supreme 'self-sacrifice' of my entombment, and its idealism, is emphasised by the absence of indulgent goods. No rich baskets of fruit, fine bottles of wine, or scented perfumes did I take with me. Not even a packet of cigarettes.

CHAPTER THREE

MY DOCTOR'S CAR boasted an expansive dashboard spattered with knobs and dials. Ordinarily these would have merely signified the amount of petrol we were carrying, the hour of the day and at what speed we were travelling. But on that ecstatically illumined day, the dashboard glittered with precious stones which entirely dazzled me. The cigarette lighter was some priceless inlaid ingot which could set fire, on a whim, to the world. The world was, however, already afire, blazing an eternal light. The windows were glazed with a trillion diamonds. We were not travelling any known road, but flying over houses and hedgerows into a land of bliss.

I remember seating myself on the concrete verge in the hospital garden while my doctor went inside the office. I was detached from the scene in much the same way as a member of a concert audience is removed from the orchestra while it is tuning up. As on such an occasion, I was interested and partly alert but not yet associated with the performers; somewhere in the back of my mind was a sense of future involvement, the ensuing music; but as I idly picked blades of grass and compared them in length to each other, I was a relaxed member of the orchestra stalls, partly interested in the programme upon my lap, but more involved, still, with the recent journey to the hall. When my doctor reappeared from the office it was as if the conductor had raised his arms to start the first bars of the concerto.

I remember the screens being arranged around the bed, the undressing and lying down to sleep. I vaguely remember a fair-haired doctor talking to me, asking questions. I think my answers were probably brusque and noncommittal. I was far too tired to enter into any conversation. I remember some medicine and a cool tumbler of water by my bed. Slowly I faded into a world of dark green screens which blurred into the darkening ceiling. The colours turned to umber, to prussian blue, the blue to black, then to darkness, a depth of no colour and infinite recession. The revelations and euphoria of the past few days, magnified to ecstatic heights by the March day and the drive through the Somerset countryside, faded into the screens and walls; I no longer floated spirally upwards, bound for the skies; my body became part of me again, I could feel its dead weight against the mattress as I passed into sleep on that Good Friday afternoon.

The pattern of my pendulum mind is strongly influenced by religious thought. I seemed to be in contact with 'that unknown source of life' which we call God. It was during this time that I felt strongly drawn to the Roman Catholic Church; it was not the first time; but it was three years before I was received into this Church, a time I used for much objective thought upon this matter and discussion with professionals. It would have been wrong to have taken immediate action during the high swing, but it was wise to utilise those lit-up days and later to link these experiences to clear and objective thought. I believe deep faith lies halfway between subjective and objective thinking. You cannot separate emotion and objective thought in matters of mystery. Thus the high swing gave me a sign upon which I could act at a later time.

I believe some of the sensations during the high flight do bear close similarities to mystical experience. The deep feeling of the unity of things, universal bliss, oneness, a sharing of everything, material and otherwise, of mystery unveiled, a sense of hidden wisdom suddenly revealed, the marrying of opposites, the non-existence of time and the evaporation of evil in the face of total goodness, all these qualities have been at some time or other professed by accepted mystics. But if it is true that there is a common meeting ground at certain levels, one must immediately admit that the egocentricity and 'lack of contact' are sure proof that these extraordinary experiences are not 'true mysticism'.

But I believe their origin is common, an intense spiritual quest after 'oneness' and the beatification of mankind.

The fundamental difference between true mysticism and the pendulum is one of course of humility. During the high swing, however near to eternal truths and revelations, one is desperately far from humility. Everything depends upon you. During the low swing of the pendulum, the sensations are completely reversed. The contrasting states are perfectly described by Wordsworth in his opening verse of his 'Ode to Intimations of Immortality from Recollections of Early Childhood'.

> There was a time when meadow, grove, and stream,
> The earth, and every common sight,
>> To me did seem
> Apparelled in celestial light,
> The glory and the freshness of a dream.
> It is not now as it hath been of yore:
>> Turn wheresoe'er I may,
>> By night or day,
> The things which I have seen I now can see no more.

When first I opened my eyes I needed to close them again to prove that I was not dreaming. This I did some half a dozen times, until the ceiling image was engraved upon my mind. It was not a deeply etched plate that laid itself across my eyes, it was a surface faintly scarred with black and grey and sudden patches of white; for there were many other scrawls across its face, worked in differing layers. A three-dimensional criss-cross-crossword puzzle vibrated behind my shuttered eyes. I opened them again. For a second I saw the ceiling as it was, grey-white with 'other white' lamp shades protruding from it, spreading left and right down the ward. Just one was dead centre above my head, perfectly curved and meaningless. On either side and ahead of me were green screens, linen with vertical folds running up and down. I was screened from the world, in a green tomb. The voices, scrapings,

6*

thuds and knocks around me were tuned to another planet. Footsteps floated, faltering for a moment, then continued with meaningless sound.

I rose from the bed and sat on its edge. There was only a bare chair beside me, nothing else. The floor was brown lino, attempting shine, succeeding only in lustre. It was cold and strange upon contact, a river with no invitation to fish it. The streams and rivers in which you fish are usually obvious, warm and welcoming. But there are just those few which have no inscription, no invitation to work with them; the one beneath my bed was of that order, coldly aloof and uncaring.

I stepped carefully into it, one foot slightly moist before the other. Then, when sure, I stood right up. I was very near the green grinning curtains. Dare I part them? Where was the gap? Where the door? Where was anything for that matter? My quarter acre was enclosed completely from the world. Only the bed seemed real and that was in the past, belonging to a million years ago. Certainly I could not return to it. I found a parting in the screens; the wheels joggled as I pushed it aside; there was a faint light ahead, a door ajar. I swayed towards this vertical strip of lighting, pasted to the dark rectangles on either side of them, then through it. THROUGH IT. It had seemed impossible a second ago. Once past it I found myself again in a sealed conclavity, all dark and wondering. There were doors and lavatories, six of them. Which should I choose? No, not number three, nor number five. Thirty-five is a multiple of seven and five and five and seven make twelve and there were twelve Disciples. I was no longer a Disciple. Directly I went to number one. This was my special prayer hole. There was a small window high up in the wall. I stood on the seat and peered out. Prussian darkness smote my face glued to the three-inch opening slit of rectangular air. I gazed into the night. Was it a garden? Was that a tree painted fiercely on to the darkness? Was that snake a path? The air bit me. It was a snake, a reptile. I lowered myself to the floor. Damp cold tiles. Another form of nasty kiss.

The journey back to bed was reassuring, not because I wanted
the shelter of those green screens, but because I knew the river
now to be the sort of lino I used to make cuts from at art school
not so very long ago.

I did not question where I was, there was no need of this. I had
been to sleep; more than that, I had been buried and was about to
rise from the dead. Meantime, I must rest a little longer in the
tomb, agree with the dark slit night pasted to the window, for all
would turn to gold on the Sunday Easter morn, all would be lit
all transformed to eternal light. I had that wand, the key to all
doors of the universe, not packed away in any suitcase, nor even
in my trouser pocket, but within me crystal clear. Why not use it
now? There was a time for all things and this was not it. I needed
no wristwatch to remind me of the hour, no clock to chime its
record, only the dark passage of time counted in drops of sweat.
Each glistening bead was a billionth minute of time risen from the
depths of hell right into my hands, up into the palms and on to
the line printed surface. I marvelled at these specks, true time-
keepers during the prussian hours. My chest was bare. Worm-
black hairs glistened there. The beads could be counted in terms of
metaphysics. I was a super-human adding machine, not counting
but multiplying in billions and finding the answer imprinted,
lower down, on my navel, one clear round nought, no more, no
less. All addition and multiplication, if reasoned to this point,
ends in infinity and the infinite is a circle, a clear round nought.
You cannot break its boundaries, only travel its perimeter or perhaps leap into its centre as I had done. Then the circle whirled
round holding me in, pin-pointed to the centre. But this pinning
to the central knob of the roulette board was not to last for ever.
All roulette boards wear out in time. First the knob comes loose,
waggles, striving to free itself from its prisonal duties, to join
the freer world at last, to bump and bounce against the 'real'
world, to break through and laugh. Laugh hugely at the gap and
look back for the slender hole, wondering that it had not happened long before. And so I spun, I the knob loosening at each

twist, ready to rattle into the open arena, striking the spinning walls; and then to break through, just once, into the open, into the world of light and song. There would be no return from the small black gap through which I would emerge. That I had rattled and banged, shuddered, shivered, shimmered, whip-cracked against those walls was of no consequence. This had been an-other world, a world filled with man-made agonies, tragedies Rembrandt etched in black; an arena filled with Rubens raptures and Rabbis wronged. The roulette world had spun its time, the walls were to be broken through; no more wailing, no more Chagall tears, no more depths of fear, only light and crystal shapes, and the music of running deer.

Lying on my bed I allowed the wheel to whirl once more; nothing could stem the spinning knob once released from its cen-tral hold, out out into the world, the world of eternal bliss. A number or two, perhaps more, might be called upon in the arena, cried out and won (and lost), grabbed and grinned over, but the time was near when I need rest no longer on chance stays (number twenty-seven?), then to another stop, this time four o one, but flame out over their grinning faces into the barrier and right through. The gleam of lightening movement would skim those faces once and for all time. For all time, eternity, out of the navel, skipping through the black worms down through the groins, out into the thighs, down the legs, into the feet and toes, up into the nails and singing to the world.

I remembered a notice I had seen which read 'Watch your Head'. Watch your head! I had thought it strange to be told to watch my head. How could you watch your head except in a glass or pane or bending low in a calm lake? And even then the water must be dark. Now I knew what those words meant. WATCH YOUR HEAD. I could watch anything I liked, low or high, mine or anyone else's. I could watch my head as easily as my feet. It was all the same, just a matter of will. 'WATCH YOUR HEAD'. One of the millions of notices ordering our lives, as if they cared. All the indifference of the world was proclaimed in those three words.

I lay still, very still, upon my bed. The time would soon be coming when these things would be changed. It would be no longer WATCH YOUR HEAD but a notice, illuminated in gold, which sang, 'We love your head, be gentle and sparing, we love so deeply your lovely head'. The words would be filled with the meaning of Christ when he spoke of the hairs on the head of a child. Each would be numbered, carefully counted; there would be corn stooks of hair blessed by the wind, golden hair and dark hair, rough dry clumps strewn to the sky imploring the world to join in the laughter. This was my will as I lay on the bed and gazed into the pale white ceiling; it was all written there. This was my will.

During the next few days the pendulum soared to Olympian heights and I was closely linked to those Athenian days of thirteen years before. I was arisen from the dead and must bless the world with the fire which had swept into me from those gesticulating stooks of corn. There was a deep compulsion to touch and heal and bless, and unite in everything. I felt a Divine gift had been bestowed upon me. I wrote furiously, as I had drawn in Greece thirteen years before. The words cascaded like stones imprisoned too long in a country wall, when the fierce grip of winter has leased its strangehold. Stone upon stone broke forth.

"There is a deep compassion within me, a flame which shoots a spark into that calm pipe-smoking man opposite, so that he is alight at the tip of his existence. The flame spurts backwards down the stem into his mouth, down the throat, into his chest, out into his thighs down into his legs and bursts forth through his feet out into his toes, from tip to toe, out of woe, through the thin window pane into the dripping, long-nailed fingers of the weeping willow which kisses the spring earth in sweetly sad embrace.

"I must snatch the glimmer from the evening air and sprinkle it upon these worn-out figures so that a new melody is born in arms and legs, in hands and hair, in bodies gutted in despair.

"There is gratitude everywhere. A bedtable leaps for joy across its care, bearing fruits of oranges and lemons, bridging me to hoops of roses. The evening sun reflects its glory in a shining trolley which fresh and white is sainted to the night.

"A matchbox standing upon its end, upon a flattened mirror, becomes a blue skyscraper rushing to the yellow sky, and this modern Gothic gesture is echoed in the upward surge of a dozen window panes.

"There are a thousand landscapes upon the lockers linked to leaves and rocks and grasses. The ashtray is an autumn heap of dying splendour, the pale yellow matches my last link with stripped wood which knows the beauty of a heart laid bare.

"I praise stripped wood with all my heart and would that I could inject its pure bare grace into the withered limbs of these tired men and thus stretch their crinkled skin to glowing youth again. Would that I could iron out those ochred wrinkles to soft pink again and marry their complexion to pale young roses.

"There was the full cascade and deafening glory of Niagara Falls in the flush of the lavatory this morning. All sin was swept away on the undercurrent flow. And through the slit-eyed window, beaming now, I saw a refuse bin so piled in glory that it filled my heart with joy. Boxes, tins and paper which man had dismissed and crumpled into an upright cylinder-fluted coffin, sang out in unison of praise, laughing and kissing close together. A wrinkled piece of paper peeped piping through, blue against a risen yellow star, which recently had been just a yellow flower. Glory rose from that round bin whose occupants had been buried for some sin.

"The wheels of the ward trolley are outward turned in comic gesture, which pleases me a lot".

"Very Early Spring.

Before Spring comes, wholly, something happens which only happens then. It is an everythingness from inside, not the bruising burst of later days. 'When Spring comes', they say, as if such a moment could be anchored to one set hour or day.

"I know it is not so. Never has been, never will be. Winter gesticulates, white embraces, branches shriek.

"Today is the love play between embrace and final unison.

"The water tap stands cool, calm, useful, just so, turns easily, sperms its flow in one short spurt. The watering can filled just too quickly. Overflow without complaint. No curse behind the splatter. The wall, no longer impressed by winter's seal, measles moss and leaf. All is well.

"Well, well, well, all is well. The well itself stands triumphant returned to ease. 'All is well, 'an it be so in t'garden,' said old John, himself an inch unbent from yesterday, his tread the same as ever, his calm unchanged. And yet did I not, for one brief moment, see him skipping, no not skipping s t r i d i n g down the gravel path, wheelbarrow flung far ahead?

"I did. I did.

"A cat is stained in early sunlight, lazing near a lavender bush. A butterfly butters by, casual is the early bee resting for a moment on a petal. Cat stretches, and yet again, all seeming peace and fun and love. Not so his panther swipe, which brings bee, to be, in one split second. Restless after such an hour of sun and shade, enquiring some new aspect or adventure like a child, the cat streaks off in fresh pursuits.

"The cat is gone. That is the point. The cat has gone. How wise, how cunning, how self sufficient, how loyal he is to his own needs, free of moral issues. The cat is gone, all else the same.

"A crow stands high upon a wall, vulture silhouette against the sky. Suddenly, swift as a jet, it swoops in angry fall. Only the twitter of smaller birds, remind of birds at all.

"Indeed this day could not be without this twitter, nor the twitter without this day.

"Oh very early Spring, so full of glory, hope and birth, a new born year, so much to come. Can we match this hour in further months, can we remember, just for one brief moment, all it meant?

"Oh very early Spring, oh very early Spring. . . ."

Everything delighted me during this high flung period. There was not anything of which I was not a part. There was a white box caught in the sunlight near my bed. A strong shadow fell towards me from it. I was both the white square box and the cool dark shadow. Black and white were one, just as good and evil cannot be separated. I knew a perfect fusion within my soul. My mind was working all the while to marry this positivity within me to the others in the ward.

I was the electric cable, the superhuman dynamo, through which all good was generated, and my task was to 'flame out like shook foil' and set the world aglow. My intent was to heal completely all those suffering in the ward.

The Concise Oxford Dictionary describes empathy as 'the power of projecting one's personality into (and so fully comprehending) the object of contemplation'. This is a matter which I have discussed in various ways in previous chapters, usually in connection with inanimate objects. But so great was this power within me during this hospital period that it broke its usual bounds and conferred itself, in an extraordinary fashion, upon people. I seemed to have the power of healing within me and needed passionately to transfer my compassion, via my fingers, to other patients. I felt sure that I could heal the most bothered patient, if only I could touch and bless him. This compulsion and compassion burned with such intensity that eventually, after I imagine many interfering attempts at solving patients' problems, I was confined to a small cell-like room off the main ward. I say 'imagine', for that intense week of 'divine duties' is obscured in memory; I merely recall the zeal and passion of my task, not the confusion that must have resulted from my attempts to cure severe schizophrenics, epileptics and other equally muddled folk. I do remember a feeling of certainty that my task had been worthwhile, though in retrospect I am sure not one of the patients benefited, unless he was particularly interested in the sorrows of the world as expressed by Rembrandt, or in the profound significance of the psalms.

One incident closely connected with this zealous work is worth recording, both for the way it illustrates the nature of the pendulum mind (when it has become 'supremo' or Christ himself), and as a reflection of our strange, surrealist, passage through this world. I must add, immediately, that I have discovered that our 'strange, surrealist passage through this world' is scarcely restricted to mental hospitals; in those places I have perhaps found extremes; but I have met far more strange and surrealist people, and events that stem from them, in the 'normal' world.

In this Somerset psychiatric hospital, confined to my cell, I was pondering, on the edge of my bed, how best I could continue healing the disturbed patients now out of my physical reach. It was quite a problem. I think my head was clasped in my hands, bent in prayer, requesting an answer to this profoundly important problem. Suddenly I heard a knock upon the door. Through the grille, I saw a face; the eyes were shining bright. The face spoke, "Oh, Master, Saviour, what is it that you command?" It was the face of a patient whom I had 'healed' only the day before. It was most gratifying to see this disciple's face, eyes radiantly shining, his nose peeping through the grille. It would have been even more satisfying to have seen his whole body. The eyes stared at me, full of adoration and subservience.

"I am thirsty," I said at last, "very thirsty." The worshipful face disappeared and there was left only the crossed bars which were a constant reminder of my responsibilities and burdens.

The face re-appeared. "A glass of water, my Saviour." The eyes shone in adoration as he softly spoke these words.

There then followed the very complicated operation of passing a tumbler of water through a grille not designed to allow such an object access. It soon became apparent that only a miracle would achieve this aim. I could sense that my disciple expected such an event, as he struggled with the tumbler at all angles which still allowed the water to remain within it. Finally in desperation, perhaps fearing the wrath of his Saviour, he angled the tumbler so that the water poured in over my feet.

When I looked up, there were just the bars staring at me.

Again the face appeared. Another glass of water glinted through the bars. Solemnly my disciple dipped in his fingers, and I sucked driblets of water through the grille, until a nurse ordered my visitor away. As he turned, he said: "Until tomorrow, my Master; then I will bring you your purple robes." With those words, I was left even more convinced of the important destiny which had been thrust upon me.

At this distance, this story is merely amusing. At that time it was a profoundly significant event and clear proof of all I was experiencing.

Two years after leaving hospital, when I was happily settled with my family (all kingships renounced), I received a letter from this patient, a fierce, hurt letter, informing me that I had betrayed 'my people', in not accepting the Messiahship; and that if I was ready to take on this heavy burden and responsibility, my robes, crown and throne would be waiting for me at Priddy.

Although I have never looked for these symbols of office in Priddy, I have often painted in that desolate Mendip village. Even before resting in hospital, I had worked there, and always I had sensed something strange and mysterious. During my stay in hospital, the countryside between Glastonbury and the Mendips, particularly Wells and Priddy, haunted me. The illusions which wove themselves around me were substantiated, in a way, by the legends which surrounded this mysterious part of Somerset; Joseph of Arimathea, the thorn at Glastonbury, the mysticism of Blake and his connection with Priddy, 'Jerusalem' ('And did those feet in ancient times'), Wells, and the strange revelations which had stemmed from working in this countryside. That the high fling of the pendulum brought illusion, I accept, of course, as fact. But some of the sensations and experiences which have resulted from working in this part of Somerset, I do not relegate to the illusionary world. They are illusionary only in the sense that I cannot prove them. But as I believe that you cannot prove most of the important matters in life, I am content to allow these experiences an important place in it. Often, working on the Mendips or in the Avalon Valley, I have sensed a mystery, not so much of unknowing, but rather, for a second, of mysterious knowingness.

While in hospital, this sensation was greatly heightened. However askew I may have been by 'normal standards', my perception was vividly awake. Alongside this heightened perception lay an inner experience closely connected to the mystic associations of Glastonbury, Wells and Priddy, whereby I felt a part of these mysteries. Again and again I felt the certainty and profundity of Blake, often in poetic images I had hitherto not understood; as the pendulum continued to swing up, so I became not only more receptive to Blake but, as it were, a very part of him. One sunlit evening we seemed to be flying hand in hand over those dark satanic mills, which for an instant were lit in sunlight, turned from their satanic darkness to glistening ivory white. We glided on together, lighting the land below us, in gestural, fitful starts, as the sun does from behind swift moving clouds.

One more incident during this period remains vividly with me. It was the last flicker of the flame, before it died down, leaving me without any warmth, passion or feeling. I remember that I was particularly elated, having met a small, quiet countryman, a fellow patient, a gardener; we had immediately formed a bond and after he had gently instructed me upon flowers and shrubs, and the ways of nature, I returned his country wisdom with a passionate discourse on superhuman nature. Some flaming flowers had fired my mind with seeming magic, and I preached with vehemence and passion.

"What is superhuman?" I cried to my gardener friend and the flowers alike, "What is superhuman, what does it mean?" I did not pause for answer; "Superhuman is human nature with a halo on; it is the ordinary, blessed by a peripheral glow, lit from within, and flaming without for all to see. Look at those flaming flowers, they dazzle like the sun and cast radiance upon all who pass by them. Indeed it is impossible to pass by, one must stop and gaze; the power of the sun hypnotises us with its hallowed blessing, in flowers and faces, trees and shrubs; the sun, and thus the halo, is everywhere; it is inside us, around us, above us, below us, turning humanity to divinity, the human to the superhuman and the whole world to an eternal glow". I spoke as I felt.

The gardener (his name was Arthur) bent forward to touch one of the crimson flowers. The gentle movement in itself seemed magical, the fusing of friend and flower.

"Ah, magic, all is magic if we allow it to be; that is where man has gone astray; he has lost contact with his primordial instincts, with nature, with the very root of himself, the very source of life; and in denying it, he has brought calamity upon himself. I know you will agree."

Arthur withdrew his hand and answered quietly: "Ah, I does agree".

"There's too much black magic," I continued, addressing a pile of discarded tins. "Black magic is magic used for wrong ends, for negative results, as a means of power and self-assertion. Magic must be white and used for positive and beneficial ends."

And so I preached that sunny summer afternoon, addressing Arthur, flowers, piles of rubble, fences, greenhouses, garden rakes and gates alike. I recorded part of this ecstatic sermon in my diary later that evening. At first the words tumbled on to the page, just as they had poured from within me while I preached to Arthur. But slowly they dried up. I was gripped by fear. The word 'gate' sprung at me from the page. The image was no longer a friendly, horizontal construction of wood, lazily leaning open against a hedgerow. It was a clear signal of distress, the cross formations of its structure reminding me of my sufferings and contradictions; suddenly the world of 'litupness', glory and eternal ecstasy, was turned to one of crucifixions and confusions; I began to experience the impotence and paralysis, the impossibility of making decisions, which was to engulf the next few weeks. Desperately, I tried to write; the palms of my hands sweated; word after word I wrote, then hurriedly crossed out; and then to make doubly sure of its cancellation, its entire obliteration, I tore the page to tiny fragments and buried them deep in the wastepaper basket. A few hours later, I emptied the basket into the lavatory bowl and flushed it several times, until I was certain my wicked words had been dispensed from this world.

I turned from my writing to the objects around me, seeking comfort in them. My friendly pipe, that would reassure me. I remember it was lying on my locker. I picked it up and with a shock saw that the last bowl I had smoked had burnt only through the centre leaving a perimeter of tobacco neatly round it. In a flash I saw myself, like the bowl, a husk surrounded by a shell. It was all written there. I looked out of the window and saw rain falling, as soft as spaniel's ears. The sadness of those gentle tears was echoed in the weeping willow. The tears were all for me, the burnt-out husk, lying flat upon my bed. I was entirely gutted.

I was a fish swimming about in the confines of a glass bowl and I knew both the surprise and inevitability that a gold fish does when he appears irregularly in sight. It was a remote and slow-motion journey with a tempo conditioned by no laws which were known to me. I was the figure in a film, talking and gesticulating while the sound is cut off, incomprehensibility and frustration bringing a silent desperation. It was a one-way traffic of communication, but so distorted and voiceless that it never reached out beyond myself.

One of my worst fears was in committing myself to anything. I had a horror of dirtying my hands, soiling my shoes, of writing letters, even of dressing myself or leaving the ward. Fear butter-flied fiercely in my stomach and often I was secluded in the lavatory for long periods. Following this act, I would wash my hands a dozen times, vainly attempting to cleanse the sins I felt needle sharp within me.

One morning I made a real effort to overcome this gripping fear. I set up my easel outside the ward. It was a fine spring morning and I was determined to dispel this ogre. I began drawing, and the rhythms started to flow; for a time I was nicely lost in the garden scene, the trees and benches, grass and paths. As I stood back from the easel, the drawing spoke to me, not in the sublime way that its spring content demanded, but in a symbolic and terrifying manner.

I discovered that the picture mainly comprised of two paths, dividing from each other, which I had scarcely noticed while I was working. They spoke to me of my divided attentions; 'Which path will you take?' they said. I was overcome with horror, for I was in no state to make such a decision. I recoiled from the drawing which so truly reflected my state of indecision. I believe it was quite an ordinary and objective drawing but at that time it reminded me of the divided world in which I was living. It was some weeks before I dared work at my painting again. I slipped back quickly to the gold-fish bowl, the silent spherical world which made no demands upon me.

The next time I remember trying to work was in a small side ward which had been put at my disposal as a studio. A spark of enthusiasm flared up in me as I set up a simple still life of oranges, apples and a bottle. I prepared my palette. It was to be an oil painting this time. Suddenly, as I took up the brushes, everything prepared for the day's work, I was filled with terror. Each stroke that I put on the canvas was quickly obliterated by another. The paint marks were frozen, meaningless, and demanded immediate cancellation. Soon the palms of my hands were sweating and I seemed to be choking; the objects grinned back in a strange and meaningless way. I fled from the room and the canvas which refused contact with a world which I so much wished to regain. Many times I returned to that small room but was never able to make headway with my painting. The room, with the deathly still easel and canvas, symbolised completely the vacuum in which I was held. The fierceness of the terror lay within me, not in the objects; nothing spoke to me and I was entirely hollow.

Again I felt this lack of contact, even more poignantly, when Dr. Hemphill invited me to his house to see his fine collection of drawings and paintings. I was delighted by this invitation and

walked almost boldly to his charming house on the edge of the
hospital grounds. There in his drawing-room were paintings that
I quickly recognised; all over the house were works which should
have meant a great deal to me. But I realised that they meant
nothing to me, nothing at all. Not one of them spoke to me and
there was not a flicker of a flame within me. It was an appalling
moment when the world I loved so dearly, the world of painting,
was completely denied to me. All grace had been withdrawn. It
was a sad and lonely journey back to the ward, a journey crowded
with doubts and fears. I had contact with nothing. Absolutely
nothing.

The pendulum was entirely still. I could see spring turning to
summer, and feel the warmth of the sun, but within me nothing
stirred except a jumbled host of self-accusations. I walked in the
fields at home with my wife, on weekend leave, in the magnificent Mendip countryside overlooking Wells, where such a
short time ago the Friesian cows and I had captured something of
its beauty. But the shimmering summer leaves and the dew-fresh
grass were entirely out of reach. I neither floated nor sank; I
merely existed. Nothing tumbled, moved or was.

Often my eyes would wander, searching the objects which I
knew and used to love so well, trying to probe, for one instant,
their noncommital air. How could that chair in the corner of our
sitting-room have once proclaimed full pride and joy? The drawing on my studio wall, of this recently joyous chair, teased me in
its lie. The proud gate, so horizontally sure of itself, had once
linked rhythmic winter hedgerows hand in hand. Gone was this
wide embrace, nor did faded yellow wisps of string echo their
dark gesticulating cousin branches. Accidental scars on walls
held no capricious beauties for there was no place for chance,
which at its birth needs movement. All was gone and I seemed
committed to this world of no existence, for eternity.

One incident, a happy one for future years, is set like a pearl
amidst the still boulders of those weeks. I went to a painting class
in the hospital art room. It was large and light and looked out

on to the fresh lawns, with shrubs and trees close by. A tall and beautiful young woman helped me to set an easel by the window. Quickly I set to work, looking through the window and translating the rhythmic trees and shrubs on to my paper. The work began to flow; then it ceased as suddenly as it had started. Something was blocking further communion with this drawing. Again I was seized with panic and fear of further committing myself. The tall young woman approached my easel and we began to talk. This was my first meeting with Barbara Fry. The tiny flame flickered when we talked of art; she told me that her husband was Tony Fry whose paintings of ecstatic dancing figures had recently meant so much to me. We discovered several mutual friends. For one brief moment the pendulum swayed. The still, 'other world' presence and beauty of Barbara, and our mutual links with the world I had lost, brought meaning to me. And then it was lost. As suddenly as it had come, as the debris on a dance floor is swept away after the dance is over, so the warmth within me faded. An outsider would still have seen two figures talking with each other, the one tall and majestically still, the other short, dark and full of nervous energy. But to me there was an impenetrable and sound-proof sheet of glass slipped between us, so that the quietly controlled tones of Barbara no longer possessed any real meaning. Subconsciously we had both made a barrier which was essential to the moment. I remember my lock gate clamping down a second after hers, in self-defence. I longed to tell her, and the world at large, that the rough coarseness of my outer self was in fact the prickly spindle of a music box; and that if correctly adjusted, the rough frozen hairs could turn to music.

Much of my stay in hospital is obliterated by the sedative drugs which I was given. Eventually it was found necessary to use 'shock treatment'; for the morning had arrived when I had been unable to get out of bed, had not the will to put on my slippers and had found it impossible to run my own bath.

I remember that particular morning with icy clarity. My feet and hands were damp and cold. The thought of the enamel bath, with its white frozen interior surface, paralysed me with fear. To enter it would be to add another frozen form to my own. I would be turned to a permanent block of ice. Firmly I stayed in my bed, relishing its warmth and security. It was a womb in which I could shelter; no doctor or nurse would wrench me from it.

I do not remember exactly how I was withdrawn from it; I think I was cajoled. But I do remember, not only the fear of the white enamel bath, but also the conflict which my feet had with my slippers. My cold and sweaty feet were terrified of further contaminating themselves by touching either the floor or the slippers. They were horrified at slipping themselves into the worn slippers, where the dirt of the world would link itself to their moisture and charge my whole system with verminous filth. I withdrew my feet in sheer horror and returned to the security of my well-tried bed.

As I have said, those 'paralysed' days are mostly hidden from me. I do not remember being particularly frightened of the 'shock treatment'. My fears lay much more deeply rooted inside me, stirred by the symbolic significance of objects and gestures. An ashtray, the angle of a pillow, the dirt on the soles of my shoes, these and their like provoked profound fear and dismay within me.

I lay on the bed waiting for the 'banger' almost with relief, relief that for an hour or so I should be cut off from this fiend-filled world of which I was such a contaminated and guilty member. My mind was rattled hysterically like dice in a thrower, its inscriptions whisked into black obscurity and then cast jumbled upon the table.

During the next few days, my mind would be fogged and jumbled as if I had been further removed from the world around me. I have no clear memories of those days. A week later (I do remember the interval), the dice would be gathered up again, rattled round and thrown for the players to re-examine.

But who were the players? Was the tall, distinguished, white-coated man one of them? Perhaps too, the grey-haired man confined to bed in the ward? Somehow I remember linking this bed-ridden man with 'the players', the investigators, the healers. Who was the man in the bed next to me? What connection had he with me? Who was anybody, for that matter?

After a few weeks this epileptic game of banging my baffled mind into another form of cloudy confusion ceased. My dice were allowed to rest again. Through the fog of those days a desperate fear haunted me, a fear that life would never again be the same. The dice had been rattled entirely out of order. Would, could, life ever allow a double six again? That was the question which throbbed constantly in my confused mind during those muddled weeks.

CHAPTER FOUR

THE LANES AND hedgerows, fields and trees still meant little to me when I was allowed home. I exchanged the confused three months of hospital for another form of jumble. There was just a faint contact with the world around me, like in an attic full of relics in a house not lived in since childhood days.

When I mowed the large lawn close to our cottage it was as if someone else was doing it. I received no pleasure from the close-cropped hair of the new green lawn and counted no satisfaction in the alternate dark and pale strips which appeared beside me. In the past the mower had converted these strips of contented carpet to measured delight. I made hay without sun, just as once bricks had been made without straw.

I returned to drawing in the orchards; but not a tree acknowledged me; if I had contact with any part of nature, it was rather in the knots upon the tree trunks than in the swelling apples and flickering leaves. Lying in the long grass under the apple trees, I wondered that the sun bothered to drop pools of light around me or illumine a particular field on the hill beyond. The change of the trees on this hill, from dark green against a light blue sky, to bright sudden yellow as the dark clouds gathered up behind, and the wand of light struck from in front, reflected an undetermined mind. There was no glory in this surprising change of light, no stab of delight as black viridian turned, in an instant, to bright greeny yellow.

I slanted diagonally and despondently down with the needle-fine rays of rain, seen through a vacant open window, and then counted my sorrows in the tears which speckled the studio window-panes. Their lack of any real intent was merged into my mind.

There was pain again in my left leg. An ulcer on the foot. Suddenly I was filled with a strong desire, stronger than any feeling I had known for weeks, to bend down my head to this ulcerous sore and suck out the pain with my mouth and lips. I would suck this oozing, stabbing sore as a snake bite is withdrawn, and leave just a neat round hole in which the air could pour.

I longed to slice my head clean through, as a knife beheads a freshly cooked egg, and scoop out all the grey muddled brains with a delicate silver teaspoon. Then I would fill it with a fresh picked cauliflower, line it with rose petals, and fix the top back on again. Sometimes I would shake my muzzy head, hard and viciously, hoping for its jumbled contents to re-assort themselves. Once I bit my tongue sharply during such an act. I was reminded of blood money and coins returned in a faulty slot machine.

A month later I still saw myself as grey and meaningless, similar to my overgrown toenails. I was filled with pity for the nails as I cut them. I thought of planting the snipped ends in some part of the kitchen garden where the dark soil might turn them into fine phallic ivory tusks. Toenails, I thought, are for ever condemned to darkness, deeply buried in the caves of shoes, and then at night quickly slipped deep down under the bed coverings. No wonder they are sad and grey and ugly. Given the light of day, they might rejoice like whiskers in a beard or dark, crisp, curly eyelashes.

It was the kitchen garden which first moved the pendulum an inch or two. I found contentment in the pale honest faces of the cauliflowers, which reminded me of grazing sheep. I rested on their placid charm. While drawing them I felt myself, for a short time, face to face with God. If God must look like anything, what better than a fine fresh cauliflower? I imagined the dry crumbly taste of a small uncooked piece of cauliflower, instead of Communion bread, with a touch of tartare sauce in place of wine.

I thought of all the things I could link with a cauliflower, honest-to-God things like sawdust, plain white cards, a child's fair hair, wooden spoons, sponges, cotton reels, dry clean linen, and a brown unvarnished soup bowl. I drew peas in their pods and knew the rush of delight which brushed them when they chased each other into a basket from the dark confinement of their green dormitories. Their contentment lay in their immaculate shape and size. I began again to sense a communion with nature.

The apples were groaning in the orchard and studding the long grass with rubies and amethysts. Wasps hollowed caves within these glistening jewels and walls held them, lazily, for a last gossip halfway between heaven and hell. I wondered whether they would reach heaven first by falling to the ground and melting into the earth, or by my consumption of them and thus pass into the world's manure heap through my aid. It was like thinking about how different I would be if my mother had married someone other than my father; if I would be 'me' at all.

There were nursery rhyme book ladders which shot diagonally into the trees, their simple patterned structure emphasising the rhythmic flow of the trunks and branches. The glow and form of Renoir was everywhere. But my pencils and paint brushes stubbornly refused to co-operate. Lurking within me was the fear of committing myself, of becoming involved with the infinite rhythms and losing myself again in the clouds. Many things were becoming right again, written on my mind, but I dared not allow them to fuse with the forces of nature.

One afternoon I was drawing an old wooden shed at the top of the orchard. Quite suddenly I began to enter it, through the drawing, and to understand its half-tone shadows. I understood so well its vacant sad half darkness. For a moment the sun lit one corner of it; a beam of glory shone from within. An ochre stretch of wood laughed in sheer pleasure at the kiss of golden light. A nail burnt fiercely blue and sharp. I was pin-pointed to the glowing beam. And then the light was gone. But a tiny flame had ignited in my brain and the dice rattled once again. Then I was spilled right out on to the long soft grass. I picked up an apple and bit hard into it, threw it to the air and kicked it thirty feet in a perfect arc directly into a waiting bucket. It shuddered round the swollen, shiny, sky-embracing golf hole, and finally was still.

There was a flashing link with the 'egg wicket' on the Greek ward wall, the 'bottle' goal beneath the bed, and the centre stump which had staggered against the wall. The curve of that rainbow kick swelled in my head, down into my chest and out into my arms and hands. I was able to draw again.

Aldous Huxley refers to the state which I have recently been describing, the low swing, as a 'negatively transfigured world'. He goes on to mention how it has found its way into literature and art from time to time, in Van Gogh's later landscapes, Kafka's stories, in the work of Gericault, and in Goya during his years of deafness and solitude. One could add other names to this list; we are much the richer for these experiences in the hands of great masters. The intention of this book has been to try and tell a little of the struggle which exists in the creative artist, particularly the deeply emotional one. A painter friend of mine, in the midst of a double tragedy which had affected his life deeply, said to me, "You see, Anthony, we must use tragedy, we must use it, make something of it, turn it from tragedy to glory". They were inspiring words which I shall long remember. Not surprisingly, they were the words of Gilbert Spencer, the fine poetic painter, and brother of the visionary Stanley Spencer. They were Spencerian words which lit the interior of his Berkshire cottage. The room was full of joy, despite the circumstances.

It is a joyous moment to turn from the darkness of the low pendulum swing, from the foreboding ward, the crouching fears and Kafkaesque shadows, to the finish of my story. In the late autumn I went to work on a lithograph at the Curwen Press in East London. I worked long hours on a large and extremely bad lithograph. Stanley Jones, who ran this excellent printing press, was always at hand to help and encourage. The horrors of the past few months faded into the lithographic inks, were stirred and mixed into blodges of colour and rolled away under pressure of the press.

Grease repels water and water repels grease. That is the principle of lithography. I understood for the first time that the fusing of negative and positive is something beyond chemistry. I had known that fusion in some strange way. Now I was back in a world which was patterned by the normal laws of chemistry. As I watched the tiny pebbles of water race fiercely away from the dark grease, I sensed again the conflict which stretches through our lives.

It was November. London was clouded in fog. There was the scent of deep winter and I journeyed home to our cottage in Somerset. Life was beginning to be good again. My daughter Annalisa was nine months old. The hedgerows were charged with the magic of winter, bristling and fiery. Gates leant resignedly between them. There were rich ploughed fields, stone walls, barns, winter elms and a waterfall not far away. The Cathedral in Wells, often shrouded in mist, proclaimed its glory. The distant, blue-grey, winter haze was suspended from the landscape foreground in the way that part of a sentence, in parenthesis, is held aloof. Christmas was approaching.

Our Christmas Tree sparkled very brightly that year. And I remember a trillion stars in the night sky. A trillion, you say? Yes, I counted them; well, perhaps there were only a billion.

> The woods are lovely, dark, and deep,
> But I have promises to keep,
> And miles to go before I sleep,
> And miles to go before I sleep.
>
> *Robert Frost*